The Wildlife of South America

THE HASTINGS HOUSE WORLD WILDLIFE CONSERVATION SERIES

THE WILDLIFE OF AFRICA

BY JOCELYN ARUNDEL

Illustrated by Wesley Dennis

THE WILDLIFE OF NORTH AMERICA

BY GEORGE FREDERICK MASON

Illustrated by the Author

The WILDLIFE of SOUTH AMERICA

By DOROTHY E. SHUTTLESWORTH

Illustrated by George Frederick Mason

Foreword by Philip K. Crowe, World Wildlife Fund

THE HASTINGS HOUSE
WORLD WILDLIFE CONSERVATION SERIES

HASTINGS HOUSE, PUBLISHERS   NEW YORK

Published simultaneously in Canada
by Saunders, of Toronto, Ltd.
Toronto 2B.

Library of Congress Catalog Card Number 66-18355

Printed in the United States of America

For JANE and JOE
who are dedicated to preserving
the beauties of our world

Contents

Foreword 9

1. Prehistoric Pageant 11

2. And Then There Were People 19

3. Through Explorers' Eyes 27

4. Tree-Dwelling Mammals 39

5. Climbers, Stalkers and Browsers 47

6. The Most Amazing Birds 57

7. In and Out of the Water 67

8. Galápagos—A Laboratory for Evolution 79

9. Where Two Worlds Meet 85

10. The Danger of Being Fashionable 97

11. While There Is Life 105

National Parks of South America 106

Bibliography 113

Index 115

Foreword

IF WILDLIFE is to survive in an already desperately crowded world, today's young people must carry on the efforts now being made by conservationists, or they may well wake up to a day when no birds sing and no animals roam the earth. The emergency is recognized at last. More than two hundred and fifty species of animals and birds are at this moment on the brink of extinction. More than fifty of these are in the United States alone, and our conservation record has been a tragic one. During the last century and a half, forty species of American fauna have become nothing more than dusty specimens on museum shelves.

South America's once rich reservoir of wildlife is in even more precarious shape than our own. During a four month's survey of that continent undertaken for the World Wildlife Fund, I was shocked to find how few people took any interest in their wildlife heritage. Of course, there are dedicated conservationists in South America who are doing their utmost to save the endangered species, but to most people, anything even faintly edible is there to be shot. Game laws exist on the books, but no one pays much attention to them, especially since enforcement is almost totally lacking.

Mrs. Shuttlesworth has done a great deal of research for this book, and in it has presented the case for conservation in South

America in appealing and simple terms. She traces the fauna of the continent from the prehistoric ages down to the present and goes into interesting detail about the various animals. Her vignettes of the great naturalists such as Darwin and Humboldt, who discovered many of the wonders of South America, make fascinating reading.

Philip K. Crowe
Executive Committee,
World Wildlife Fund

1

Prehistoric Pageant

WHEN THE EARTH was very young, there was no life on it; it was a world of barren rock. Many long ages passed before even the most primitive forms of plants and animals came into existence. Then more ages rolled by before there was an abundant animal population.

No one was present to record these early steps of creation. People who could chronicle history were very late arriving on the scene, but the earth's story was constantly being written just the same. Fossils were forming as bones turned to stone, and plants and animals left their impressions in the rocks that were taking shape. Today, through these rocks and fossils, man can read about prehistoric times.

As one follows the many events that occurred during the earth's early formative years, it is possible to see how land areas sometimes disappeared under the restless oceans, perhaps to reappear later, and how continents took shape. On this changing earth there was at one time a gigantic chain of islands, with mountainous peaks rising thousands of feet in the air. As rain and wind beat against the slopes, these were gradually worn down and the channels between the islands built up until eventually there was a continuous land formation—South America in the making. Later this continent was shaped into two parts as the Andes Mountains formed a division between east and west. It is believed that the eastern portion was joined to Africa, but eventually the Atlantic Ocean cut through the great land mass, dividing eastern South America from Africa. A large part of the continent west of the Andes sank beneath the Pacific Ocean.

As the earth in its upheaval thrust the Andes from ocean bottom into a lofty mountain range, a narrow strip of land to the north—the Isthmus of Panama—was also raised above the water's surface. This became an important bridge between South America and North America, over which animals, and later people, could travel from one continent to the other.

The Animal Kingdom Is Established

After some millions of years of development, a fabulous parade of animal life began on the earth in many different places. In the waters, little jelly-like blobs came into being, then creatures with shells, then fishes. A tremendous change occurred when animals left the water for the first time, crawling onto dry land. After them appeared reptiles of endless variety, then the mammals. Along the way, too, insects developed, and dragon-like reptiles took to the air in time to be succeeded by birds. Man was the ultimate creation.

What an exciting pageant! Man's coming into a world already teeming with life might have seemed rather unimportant at first, for the earliest peoples shared woodland and plains peacefully with the animals, as all struggled to find food on an equal basis. It seemed that man was not really changing anything.

However, man was destined to become the earth's master. He invented weapons that gave him power over animals far larger and stronger than himself. He could kill them in self-defense; he could kill them as a source of food and clothing. In time some animals, such as wild dogs, learned to accept people as friends; others, agreeable to domestication, lived side by side with their masters. Man could be kind to wildlife, or he could destroy it, but whichever his inclination, he controlled its fate.

Prehistoric Mysteries

Happily, man developed the ability to write, and many of his thoughts and actions during the past few thousand years are on record for all to read. When the greatest of all records, the Bible, was written, people were already mindful of the importance of animals. *Genesis,* the ancient chronicle of creation, includes the story of how Noah took a male and female of every sort of creature into the ark that they might be saved from the Flood; and of how, when the waters receded, he went forth bringing "birds and animals and every creeping thing that creeps upon the earth."

Since then animals have been written about countless times— in wonder, in admiration and, more recently, in growing concern for their survival. With this concern, it is important to look backward at the prehistoric scene, trying to discover clues as to why certain animals ceased to exist, for with all the discoveries that have been made, there are still many mysteries.

One puzzle yet to be solved is why those fascinating reptiles, the dinosaurs, completely vanished from the earth. During the Mesozoic Era (often called the Age of Reptiles), they populated all the great continents. South America had its share. On some parts of the continent towards the end of the era, there was Ankylosaurus*—not a gigantic dinosaur, but impressive because of its arched back and a body encased in armor. Roaming through the lush, swampy vegetation were the sauropod dinosaurs. These were huge but quite defenseless. They had no armor. Their teeth were suited only for plant eating.

---

* Ankylosaurus is capitalized because it is the name of a specific dinosaur; sauropod (in the next sentence) has a small letter because it names a kind of dinosaur.

There are several theories as to why these and all other dinosaurs became extinct. It may be that their disappearance was concerned with changing climates as, in many parts of the world, the warm, tropical air was replaced by fluctuating temperatures. This would have put the cold-blooded beasts, slow and ponderous as they must have been, at a disadvantage in competing with the very active, warm-blooded mammals that were coming into prominence. Problems must have been created for the dinosaurs, also, when tropical lowlands with abundant palms gave way to uplands with hardwood forests. Tropical vegetation had been the food of the herbivorous species, while the carnivorous species ate the plant-eaters.

None of these theories, however, nor any other yet formulated, is entirely satisfying to scientists. Turtles and crocodiles also lived during the Age of Reptiles, but they have survived to the present. Why, then, did not a single kind of dinosaur carry on through the Age of Mammals?

Another prehistoric mystery concerns the camels. During the Cenozoic Era, which followed the Mesozoic, when mammals had become well established, this family had its beginnings in North America, with ancestors no larger than jack rabbits. Later, primitive camels about the size of sheep roamed all over the grassy plains of the North American continent.

These early camels prospered, increasing in numbers and varieties, and after many generations they began to migrate from their original home. Some went north and westward, crossing into Asia. Others wandered southward through Mexico and across the Isthmus of Panama, and then spread out through South America. Ages later guanacos, descendants of the early camels, were found there by Spanish explorers. By that time on the North American continent, the place of their origin, there were no camels of any kind.

ANKYLOSAURUS

The survival of horses, or the lack of it, presents the same sort of mystery as that of the camels of prehistoric times. Fossil evidence shows that the earliest primitive horses lived on the North American continent. There were some in Europe, too, but in time the primitive horses of the Old World died away, while in North America they not only survived, but increased in number and varieties. Eventually the true horses developed. They had, among other features, the single toe, or hoof, on each foot. Long-legged and built for speed, these horses could outrun enemies and easily get to new grazing grounds if grass became scarce. They roamed in great herds over the plains.

Then came the glaciers! The great ice sheets edging down from the north to the United States area presumably brought great hardship to the animals. At any rate, it was at the beginning of the Ice Age that the American horses began to migrate. A number went southward to South America. Others crossed into Asia. Some descendants of these migrants kept going as far as Europe and even on into Africa. Like the camels, horses ceased to exist in their original homeland. In South America, too, they died out, not even leaving descendants, as the camels had done in the form of guanacos. But thousands of years later when Europeans brought horses back to the new world, they flourished—especially those that escaped domesticity to lead a natural life.

The Giants

Some time after horses and camels had become established on earth, there was a period during which many giant mammals came into existence. One that lived on the South American plains and prairies was the ground sloth called *Megatherium* or "great beast." This monster was as large as an elephant, with long, coarse hair. It could rear up on its thick hind legs to a height of nearly twenty feet. Megatherium was not a menace to other animals, however. It ate only leaves. Sitting in a semi-upright position, it pulled branches forward, then curled its long, prehensile tongue around the masses of foliage and drew them into its mouth.*

Another South American animal of the past was *Glyptodon* or "grooved tooth," a relative of today's armadillo. Glyptodon, though looking much like a gigantic turtle, was a mammal. Its shell, made up of numerous small bones, was five or six feet in length. Bony rings covered part of a heavy tail which ended in a spiked club. The animal could not roll its body into a ball as modern armadillos can, but would crouch on the ground, with its head close to its shell, when a possible enemy came near.

---

* Many of the habits, as well as the appearance, of extinct animals can be deduced from their fossilized remains. In the case of Megatherium, massive hind limbs and a muscular back indicate the animal sat in an upright position. Its teeth and jaws show it was herbivorous; its long forelegs with enormous claws reveal that it must have reached out to secure branches for its food.

One kind of enemy it had to watch for was the sabre-toothed cat, or tiger, ever on the alert for meat. The cat, *Smilodon* or "carving-knife tooth," was as large as a lion, with powerful shoulders and muscular legs. Eight-inch long fangs enabled it to stab and slash its victims—even those as large as Megatherium.

Typically South American were the *Toxodonts* or "bow tooth." Nearly all their known fossil remains are from this continent. The toxodonts varied in size. Some kinds were small. Others were all of ten feet long. The massive body of the larger type suggested a rhinoceros, but the face was more like that of a giant guinea pig. Toxodonts could walk on land, though their pace must have been slow; their usual habitats were swampy lakes and rivers.

Such were a few of the great mammals that inhabited South America when the Cenozoic Era—which had lasted for sixty million years—drew to a close. Along with these and many smaller mammals, the reptiles and amphibians, birds and insects, also flourished. This was indeed a rich land for man to inherit.

TOXODONT

2

And Then There Were People

FAR AWAY FROM South America, on the Asiatic continent, the human race was growing and expanding. To a great extent the people depended on game for food, and had developed weapons for hunting, such as clubs and spears. Fish often gave variety to their diet, and so did wild fruits and edible seeds, but meat was of utmost importance. As they improved their weapons and learned to cook meat so that it could be kept for those times when game was scarce, animals often were not plentiful enough to satisfy the demand for them. Family groups, therefore, did not settle in one place; they roamed far and wide after the herds.

It was about fifteen thousand years ago that some of these nomads found themselves at the northeastern coast of Asia. Before them lay the Bering Strait—a narrow, shallow body of water which, in that region, was all that separated Asia from North America. Small islands rose from it, like stepping stones. When the water froze, ice formed a solid bridge between the two continents.

The hunting groups—for the most part a Mongoloid type with bronze-color skin—must have paused for some time on their side of the icy link between two lands. They had no way of knowing that a new world, uninhabited by people, lay ahead, but they saw game animals moving in that direction, and eventually this was all the encouragement they needed. They set out toward the unknown.

Citizens for a Varied Land

These early explorers must have found the wildlife plentiful and the hunting good, for they did not turn back. Some kept to the north while others turned southward, following the same route by which a number of Old World animals had already passed to new grazing grounds. Eventually various family groups reached the Isthmus of Panama and crossed it into South America. Again they fanned out in different directions, and to all corners. Even the Patagonian area in the far south—dry, barren and cold—received its share, and Tierra del Fuego, at the very tip, also had settlers.

In the course of time, there were some forty tribes established on the continent. The development and success of these people depended to a great extent on the climate in the various areas, on the opportunities for good hunting and on their skill in growing food.

Today the continent is divided into ten republics and the three colonies of Guiana. According to its natural divisions, it has four main regions: a narrow desert area on the western coast, the Andean mountain range, the foothills to the east, and the valleys and plains drained by the rivers. The Amazonian drainage basin is the greatest of these.

It was in the high Andean plateau that the civilization of the Incas developed. Along with their remarkable talent for working in gold and silver, they displayed skill in handling animals and in farming. They domesticated guinea pigs, alpaca and llama—and these two descendants of prehistoric camels were treasured for many uses. The llamas were excellent beasts of burden; their coarse wool and skin provided warm clothing; their flesh was a constant meat supply; their dried manure could be burned as fuel. The wool of the alpaca was used for finer clothing. Vicuña, which did not become domesticated, were hunted for their beautifully silky hair, but its use was limited to providing garments for the royalty of the empire.

ALPACA

Long before the coming of Europeans, the Incas had invented looms for weaving, learned to irrigate dry land for farming and constructed terraces in the sides of steep slopes. They built excellent stone roads and rope suspension bridges and made metal knives and axes. It was in this state of development that Pizarro and his warriors found the Incan Empire. When the Spaniards moved in, making the land and people their own, changes quickly came about. The Conquistadors had no appreciation of the Incas' remarkable enterprise. They enslaved the Indians, and devoted all their energies to a feverish search for gold. The carefully wrought farming terraces fell into disrepair and plentiful food supplies disappeared. But one thing the invaders did not change was the dependence of the Incas upon llamas. Today these animals are still the principal beasts of burden. It is estimated that some seven hundred thousand are in use among the Indians.

Life in the Jungles

Eastward from the Andes Mountains, a number of spurs jut out, thrusting their way into the jungle. Many of their slopes are covered with forests where animals can flourish. Some areas have rich soil—good agricultural land—which supports a number of Indian people. Among the wildlife are weasels and chinchillas, and the native Indians have shown considerable ingenuity in the use of these animals. Desiring the chinchillas for their exquisitely soft fur, they tame the grisons—a type of weasel—and teach them to flush out the little mouselike creatures, which are then easily captured.

Below the intermediate land of the mountain spurs, lie heavily forested lowlands with broad waterways, which spread through the Amazon jungles. This is a realm that may best be described as "indescribable." It is the largest and most continuous tropical forest

CHINCHILLAS

LLAMAS

left in the world, and because of its forbidding nature, it is almost completely untouched by so-called civilizing influences. Its inhabitants include a fantastic variety of wildlife and some groups of Indians who live much as their ancestors did for many centuries.

The forest Indians are inventive. Not having flint or obsidian for making cutting tools, they learned to fashion these necessities of fish teeth, bamboo slivers, fibrous palm wood and polished stone. They use bows and arrows skillfully, and hunt animals for food and for ornamental dress. The gaudy feathers of such birds as macaws are prized for making impressive headdresses.

Many of these Indians know how to make good use of plant life. Not only do they eat wild fruits and berries, they cultivate manioc for its roots, which form a staple food, and they plant such crops as beans and maize. They have been doing this for generations, but with no understanding of conservation, and after a while, even in this land of abundance, the unhappy results of a slash-and-burn method of agriculture have begun to show. Because overland travel was so difficult, everyone chose to live close by the rivers, and it was inevitable that the narrow zone along the banks, which took the brunt of the farming, would become barren and unproductive. When that happened, the people moved to a new location —and the destructive cycle began again. This procedure is still followed.

Thus goes jungle life in South America—yesterday and today, varying not very greatly in the forested parts of Brazil, Colombia, Venezuela and the Guianas. Some of the natives have been friendly to explorers from the outside world. Others have showed savage hostility to strangers. But it has not been native opposition that has caused these lush, green regions to remain unconquered by agriculturists, commercial interests, or adventurous settlers from other lands. It is the jungle itself—a solid mass of vegetation that defies the kind of pioneering that opened up the woodlands of North

America. As soon as trees and thick vines are cleared, they are ready to creep back again; an endless fight against them is necessary. Single families or small groups of people are not able to cope with the struggle.

Changes are coming, however. Landing fields allow airplanes to come down in places formerly inaccessible. A journey from Rio de Janeiro to the center of the Amazon Basin used to take months. Today the same trip is accomplished by air in eight or nine hours. The time is coming when large-scale commercial enterprises will find a way to take over, remodeling this amazing area so that it conforms to today's aim of making everything produce for a profit. This is when its unique wildlife may be lost forever. Fortunately there are people alert to the coming crisis. One organization working to protect South American animals is the World Wildlife Fund. You will read about its activities in Chapter 9.

Primitive Hunters of Today

In Tierra del Fuego, a group of bleak islands which politically are a part of both Argentina and Chile, are people who live amid wildlife much as their ancestors did a few thousand years ago. The name of the area, meaning "Land of Fire," may have originated because of the natives' use of torches when hunting birds at night. The people are the Ona or "Foot" Indians .

The Ona are hunters; their chief prey is the guanaco, and their method of attack is one kind of prehistoric hunting that has survived to modern times. Hunting teams of possibly five or ten men set out before dawn with their equipment of bows and arrows and disguises—the disguise being a headdress of white fur, resembling the forehead of a guanaco. First, game must be located, and to do this the hunters spread far apart. To keep in touch with one another, they work out signals resembling bird calls which will not catch the attention of their intended victims. When guanacos are found, the men who are wearing disguises infiltrate the herd from the rear and drive the animals toward their companions who stand ready with bows and arrows. Some of this hunting is now simplified because the hunters have learned to use dogs, training them to scent out the guanaco and bring it to bay.

The climate of Tierra del Fuego is severe, and without the guanaco, the Indians there surely could not survive in their primitive state. The animal skins furnish a simple shelter against wind and the rain, sleet and snow that fall through much of the year. They also are turned into sturdy capes and moccasins for use in the most severe weather; bags for carrying water are also fashioned from them. Guanaco meat is the sustaining food of the Ona.

Here is man's dependence on wildlife in its simplest form—as it was before such animals as domesticated sheep, cattle and birds brought food and clothing supplies into the scope of big business. Today, for the most part, the world's wildlife is not needed for practical purposes. It serves, instead, to arouse man's wonder at nature's inventiveness, and to keep on earth the marvels of "every living beast and bird" which took so many millions of years to evolve. Man, too, has been inventive, but unfortunately a number of his inventions, beginning with the gun, have wrought great havoc in the animal kingdom.

3

Through Explorers' Eyes

DURING THE EIGHTEENTH century, despite such shattering events to claim their attention as the French Revolution and the conquests of Napoleon, many Europeans were fascinated by the tales they heard of South America. Some were fired with ambition to explore the continent—among them Alexander von Humboldt.

Humboldt, a German of noble birth, was one of the pioneers in discarding old, unproved theories about the earth and its creatures. Since boyhood he had read about South America and dreamed of going there. He was in his mid-twenties when his mother died, freeing him to leave his homeland. Traveling to Paris, he found the most noted scientists of Europe. As he lived among them, exchanging ideas and questions, he was constantly looking for an opportunity to leave for the New World. Several hopeful connections failed to materialize, but finally he met Aimé Bonpland, an enthusiastic young botanist, and the two men joined forces to achieve their ambitions. They journeyed to Spain, crossing the Pyrenees on muleback, and at long last made contact with King Charles IV, in search of passports which would give them freedom to enter and roam at will over the fabulous Spanish territories in South America. The year was 1799 when Humboldt's dream began to be realized, and he left Europe with Bonpland.

The enthusiasm of these two men for the project seems incredible: Hipolito Ruiz, a Spaniard who shortly before had returned from an expedition to Peru, described at length his tortures from heat, hunger, thirst, tempests, earthquakes, plagues of mosquitoes and gnats, and constant dangers from jaguars, bears and savage Indians. And while Humboldt was living in Paris, he heard told and retold the dreadful story of Isabela de Godin who had been lost for weeks in the Amazon jungles, and who finally reached civilization more ghost than human—the only one of more than a dozen people to survive the ordeal.

No such accounts, true as he knew them to be, daunted Alexander Humboldt. As his passport stated, he was "traveling for the acquisition of knowledge." So, on a fine May day, the short, energetic explorer turned his keen gray eyes toward the Atlantic Ocean and the western horizon. His ship, *El Pizarro*, was setting sail. He was twenty-eight years old, and at last he was on his way to South America.

Humboldt Explores the "Earthly Paradise"

Humboldt's primary purpose was to follow the Orinoco River to its source and to discover where it and the Amazon made connections. But he and Bonpland arrived in the New World at the mouth of the Rio Orinoco during the rainy season, and temporarily postponed this venture. Instead they began a fantastic collecting spree, concentrating on birds, insects and plants. They could scarcely believe their eyes, so tremendous was the wealth of wildlife and vegetation in the savannas, jungles and rivers. Next they turned their attention to the llanos of Venezuela. At the time these flat, almost treeless plains were in the midst of their dry season when they strongly resemble a desert. In the wet season they are pleasantly green, with a covering of short grass, but Humboldt found the grass like chalk. He wrote, "even the alligators and snakes remain buried in the dried mud until awakened by the first showers." Amazing that the animals and plants could ever spring to life again!

In the streams that cut through the llanos, an exciting form of life was discovered: electric eels. Humboldt was first told about them by the Indians. Then he saw their terrific power when a horde of them swarmed out of the mud to attack horses that waded into the stream for a drink. The electric shocks were strong enough to knock down the big animals. The explorers managed to bring some eels upon the bank, and accidentally Humboldt stepped on one.

"I do not remember," he wrote later, "a more dreadful shock than that which I experienced. I was affected during the rest of the day with a violent pain in the knees and in almost every joint."

He found that an eel's usual behavior was to lie quietly at river bottom. When disturbed, it gave off heavy discharges, arousing other eels in the vicinity which also began to send out shocks. Since water is an excellent conductor, it soon sparkled with electrical force. An animal subjected to this is quickly stunned, and becomes an easy victim to the shocking eels.

Despite the many evidences of nature's harshness in this strange land, Humboldt agreed with Columbus, who had marked the area of Venezuela as "Earthly Paradise" almost three hundred years earlier. When Humboldt and Bonpland finally returned to the swirling waters of the Orinoco, they were enchanted. Already they had seen greater variety in animal life than they had ever dreamed of in Europe, but here was even more and in quantity.

"Animals of different nature," Humboldt wrote, "succeeded one another. Alligators appeared on the banks. Motionless, with their mouths open, while by them and near to them capybaras, the large web-footed rodents that swim like dogs and feed on roots, appeared in bewildering herds, even lying among the alligators, seeming to know that these repulsive animals do not attack on

CAPYBARA AND TAPIR

land. Tapirs broke through the tall grass and slipped down to the Apure (River) to drink."

As Humboldt and Bonpland progressed along the Orinoco River, they saw that the terrain on either side was rougher, with the flat llanos giving way to sheer cliffs and gigantic rocks. The river waters became swift and turbulent, and they had increasing problems with their strange sailing vessel—a reconstructed thirty-foot dugout canoe. However, four Indian paddlers kept the craft going.

Insects were an enemy that even the dauntless Humboldt could not dismiss lightly. There were the *piumes,* small enough to pass through the eye of a needle. These stung like wasps and drew blood with their bites. Mosquitoes, gnats, flies, chiggers and ants

CROCODILES

also were ever-present. But there was no retreat. Bonpland escaped from the insect hordes long enough to press his plant specimens by crawling into a large oven which friendly Indians allowed him to use.

At last the destination was reached—Humboldt's long-time dream was realized. He stood at the banks of the little Casiquiare River, which joins the two great river systems of the Amazon and Orinoco. In the following months he was busy making remarkably accurate maps and charts that were to dispel forever many of the fantasies that had existed about this land. But he was never so absorbed with the work that he failed to delight in the wildlife. In the heart of this jungle paradise he wrote, "Every object declares the grandeur of the power, the tenderness of Nature, from the boa constrictor which can swallow a horse, down to the hummingbird balancing itself on a chalice of a flower."

Actually Humboldt's "discovery" of South America was just beginning. He was to spend three long years on the continent, exploring the land that forms the present countries of Venezuela, Colombia, Ecuador and Peru. Later he was to have a great influence for good in the living standards of the under-privileged of South America, and was to write many volumes on its geology, astronomy, vulcanology and archaeology.

Charles Darwin's Voyage

"The day has been frittered away in obtaining the passports for my expedition into the interior. It is never pleasant to submit to the insolence of men in office . . . but the prospect of wild forest, tenanted by beautiful birds, Monkeys & Sloths & lakes by Cavies & Alligators, will make any Naturalist lick the dust. . . ."

The impatient young man who penned this complaint in his diary was Charles Darwin, young English naturalist, waiting in Rio de Janeiro to cut through the governmental red tape of Brazil so he could start exploring. The year was 1832. Thirty years had passed since Alexander Humboldt left South America, and his *Personal Narrative,* published during those years had influenced Charles from the time he learned to read. Resisting all career plans made for him by his family, he collected shells, minerals and insects—and read about South America. Humboldt was his idol.

Charles was twenty-one, a tall handsome youth, when the chance of a lifetime came. A small ship, the *Beagle,* was to leave for Tierra del Fuego. The main objective of the trip was to make soundings and measurements around the southern tip of South America, but it was considered worthwhile to add a naturalist to the ship's company. Young Darwin was offered the post. Family opposition finally overcome, he was ready to begin the great adventure of making his own personal acquaintance with the fabulous continent which he knew only through reading. Now the *Beagle* lay at anchor in the harbor at Rio, and he was being detained with passport technicalities.

Soon even this last small barrier to his ambitions was disposed of; Darwin was on his way to South American exploration. The area he approached lay not far behind Rio. With a group of five companions he rode on horseback into the heavy mass of vegetation and, as he recorded in his diary, he "was at an utter loss how sufficiently to admire the scene" as shafts of sunlight cut through the tangled mass of vegetation. On they went into the night, when gayly colored parrots and toucans were replaced by swooping bats. This scene was equally pleasing to the young naturalist.

Two weeks spent in this, his "first jungle," was an educative period for young Darwin. By the time he again boarded the *Beagle*, his powers of observation had been sharpened, his mental capacities strengthened and deepened. As the *Beagle* headed southward toward Patagonia, he noted in his diary that he was "full of expectation & interest about the undescribed coast of Patagonia. Endless plans are forming for catching Ostriches, Guanaco, Foxes, etc. Already in our day-dreams have we returned heavily loaded with Cavies, Partridge, Snipes, etc."

But when they reached Patagonia, it was not the living birds and beasts that sent Darwin into a frenzy of excitement. It was a rich deposit of fossil bones, protruding from a reddish clay bank. There was the giant ground sloth, Megatherium, a Toxodont, armadillos, and an animal with a neck like that of a camel. Some bore a strong resemblance to creatures of the present day; others were more strange. All were giants. As Darwin examined them he was sure they were skeletons of extinct animals and in his keen mind there formed the germ of an idea that would soon shake the scientific world: evolution.

When the *Beagle* was ready to start north again, Darwin asked permission to travel by land, meeting the ship at Buenos Aires. With a gaucho guide, he set off on horseback to cross four hundred miles of pampas. There he was able to enjoy weeks of wildlife study, without the slightest interruption from people. Countless guanaco, deer, skunks and armadillos roamed fearlessly around him. He was fascinated by rheas, the great, flightless birds which he persisted in calling "ostriches." He tried to check stories he had been told about the hunting habits of pumas. These big fawn-colored cats, it was said, lay in wait at the top of short ombu trees, alert for prey. When an animal came below, the puma would spring, dig its claws in the victim's back, then deliberately raise a paw and bring it down, breaking the creature's neck. Darwin saw a number of pumas, but only at a distance. However, he examined the skeletons of many guanacos lying on the pampas and found that without a doubt their necks had been dislocated.

Darwin particularly admired the guanacos. He wrote of one, "an elegant animal—with its long slender neck and fine legs," and he delighted to see herds of them running across the pampas side by side with the rheas. He knew that in ancient times this member of the camel family had been valued for its wool by the people of the Andes, but it never had become a beast of burden as had its relative, the llama. He found guanacos plentiful. They ranged from Bolivia to Tierra del Fuego; sometimes there were as many as several hundred in a single group.

The end of his solo trip to Buenos Aires was made on the Rio de la Plata where he was able to enjoy watching varied birdlife.

DARWIN AND RHEAS

Snowy-white egrets, roseate flamingoes, kingfishers—there was winged beauty all along the way.

The *Beagle*, with Darwin once more on board, now turned southward. Excitement again was high. This time the destination was Tierra del Fuego. Here, with the Ona and related tribes living much as their primitive ancestors had done, it would be like a visit to the Stone Age.

The natives fulfilled the explorers' expectations of discovering a different world, but Darwin found only scanty wildlife in the rugged climate. Besides guanaco, he saw nothing but a bat, a few mice, some deer and foxes. Birds were scarce, too; there were no reptiles. He was consoled, however, by the waters around the islands which teemed with fish, whales and seals. He could study them all at close range.

The adventures went on. Years passed. Sometimes with the *Beagle* as his headquarters, often on foot or muleback, Darwin explored South America. In Chile he climbed the Andes to such heights that he was overcome with mountain sickness. Then a glimpse of thousands of small fossils, exposed in the rocks, provided a quick cure. He made notes on the changing scene in some areas. In Argentina, he wrote, "Few countries have undergone more remarkable changes, since the year 1535, when the first colonists of La Plata landed with seventy-two horses. The countless herds of horses, cattle and sheep, not only have altered the whole aspect of vegetation, but they have almost banished the guanaco, deer, and ostrich."

As the *Beagle* finally left the shore of Peru, a great circle had been completed: Alexander von Humboldt and Charles Darwin, between them, had circumnavigated the entire continent. This was an important milestone, but Darwin's greatest discoveries and observations were still to be made. The *Beagle* was headed for the Galápagos Islands where birds and giant reptiles would enable him to unravel many of the mysteries of evolution.

The Twentieth Century Scene

Following the publication of Darwin's *Voyage of the Beagle* in 1839 and *Origin of Species* twenty years later, there was a lively interest in South America among scientists of Europe and the United States. And as the nineteenth century drew to a close there was also feverish activity among big business corporations concerning the continent. Machines were introduced for all kinds of enterprises; railroads were stretched over pampas and even into some jungles; ships sailed regularly up the Amazon. Nevertheless, there were still many areas that could be marked "For hardy explorers only."

And there still were hardy explorers who pioneered in the tradition of Humboldt and Darwin. One was Richard Spruce of England, who trekked through the Amazon jungle for seventeen years, making botanical collections. In other countries zoological societies and museums organized expeditions to study fauna and flora in South America.

An outstanding twentieth century scientist-explorer who devoted much of his time to that continent was William Beebe. Some of his earliest expeditions took him there, and then, after a variety of other earth studies—the heights of the Himalayas, the depths of the ocean—he returned again. The year was 1945. Nothing could more quickly point up the changes that had taken place since the times of Darwin than the fact that his exploring was in the *National Park* of Aragua! The wilderness was still there—but it was "under guard" due to the good efforts of the Venezuelan government. "Legislation," Dr. Beebe wrote, "has saved intact an area of quite untouched, primitive jungle." Nevertheless, from his headquarters at Rancho Grande in the Park he could see the ravages of drastic erosion caused by forests having been cut away and goats grazing on the land. Many slopes were quite bare. Evaporation from a once beautiful lake had become rapid and the inflow to it from streams was slow. The lake had shrunk to a fraction of its former size.

As he looked over the scene, Dr. Beebe may well have given a thought to the ancient Incas who prevented erosion by building mammoth terraces. This practice was one reason for the greatness of their civilization.

During the course of the three separate expeditions made by Dr. Beebe and his staff to Rancho Grande, they studied minutely the wildlife of this one section of the Venezuelan Andes, for they were interested in the total picture of animals and plants in a given area. Monkeys, bats, vultures, egrets, boas, coral snakes, tree frogs, giant grasshoppers, butterflies, ants, spiders—these and all their allied fellow-creatures were closely observed and later described in scientific papers. Dr. Beebe, besides, wrote numerous articles and books which added to a popular interest in South American wildlife.

The Amazon area of central Brazil became a particularly strong magnet for natural science explorers. In 1943 the Central Brazil Foundation sponsored an expedition to make a thorough study of it, and Dr. Helmut Sick was in charge of its science research. As he deplored the state of many rural areas where forests had been destroyed to make room for plantations, and where animal life was fast disappearing, he welcomed the opportunity to see Brazil's unspoiled green wilderness. The expedition lasted several years during which Dr. Sick became acquainted with an endless variety of animals. He collected specimens for his zoological studies but, besides this, he acquired many living birds, mammals, amphibians and insects which the Indians brought to him as pets. His book, *Tukani* and his published reports give vivid descriptions of territory completely unknown before the expedition, and of its unique wildlife.

Photographers and collectors from zoos have made many a trek to the Brazilian forests as well as to other parts of South America, and they continue to do so. The riches of scenery and animals still make it a paradise for their kind of hunting. This is a good kind which does not endanger any species, and which allows arm chair explorers back home to share in the wonders of a fabulous land.

4

Tree-Dwelling Mammals

MAMMALS—THE FURRED and hairy beasts, both large and small—
seem to belong on the ground. Trees appear a more suitable habitat
for birds and insects.

But not in South America! On this continent of the unexpected, a tree is as likely to shelter a large, hairy mammal as it is
a perching bird. The shaggy sloth, often pictured hanging upside
down from a branch, is only one of them. Monkeys, silky anteaters,
kinkajous, even some rats and mice, are a few of the others that
spend a great part of their time high off the ground.

Sloths and Armadillos

A life in the trees is not the only strange feature of sloths.
Their upside-down position is another: they can eat that way,
sleep, mate and bear young. However, during the hot hours of the
day a sloth often stretches out on its back against one part of a
forked branch with forearms clasped across its chest or behind
its head. It keeps from falling by anchoring its hind feet to the
second branch of the fork. The sloth also is a curiosity of nature
in having the yellowish hairs of its coat filled with tiny pits in which
minute algae live. These are bright green during wet seasons, causing the sloth's fur to appear green. When the vegetation is dry, the
algae turn brownish—and so do the sloths. In each case the animal
is well camouflaged.

Besides being camouflaged, sloths derive protection from natural enemies by the way they hang from branches. It is difficult for a puma to get at a body suspended in such a position. Sloths also are extremely tough, and can survive injuries that would kill almost any other vertebrate. If attacked, they are capable of dealing a vicious blow; they have a large, curved claw on each "hand." With these aids to survival the sloths have done well, for they still flourish in the rain forests of South America in spite of looking like something from the prehistoric world. However, where extensive tree-cutting takes place for projects such as airplane landing strips, they suffer great losses.

Anteaters, close relatives of the sloth, are at home both in the trees and on the ground. The giant anteater—the species with the magnificent bushy tail—can climb, and hoist its six or seven foot length up a large trunk without difficulty. Mostly it stays on earth, however, hunting ant or termite nests, which it can easily rip open. Even a concrete-hard termite structure cannot long withstand the anteater's gigantic claws. Once an opening has been made, the animal sticks its pointed nose into the nest and flicks up the insects

GIANT ANTEATER

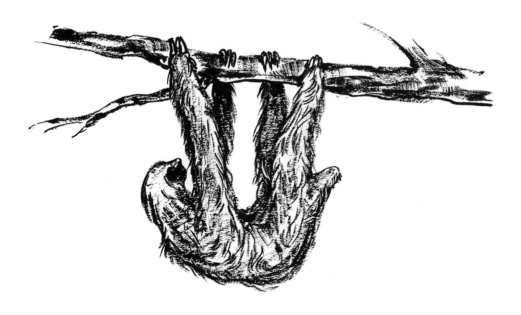

SLOTH

on its foot-long, wormlike tongue covered with gummy saliva. At times it may use its tail to sweep together a collection of insects, the better to eat them. The tail also serves as a covering blanket, curled over the creature's head and shoulders as it sleeps.

The lesser anteater is somewhat smaller than the giant and its tail is almost naked. It spends about half its time in the trees and is a skillful and rapid climber. The silky anteater, the least familiar member of the family, lives in the rain forests from Paraguay to Mexico. A beautiful, fluffy animal with golden-yellow fur, it is about the size of a squirrel.

Also related to sloths and anteaters are the unbelievable armadillos. Most of those that remain in the world today are found in Brazil, Bolivia and Argentina, in a variety of surroundings, from grasslands to equatorial forests. With an armadillo, a coat of armor takes the place of hair or fur. On top of the head is a small shield, and the tail is covered with either bony rings or plates. There are about a dozen different species. The giant armadillo is the most extraordinary. An adult may weigh a hundred pounds or more, and despite its heavy armor it can stand straight upright and walk on its hind legs, unsupported.

In contrast to this giant is the fairy armadillo—only five inches long from snout to tail tip. Long hair grows on its flanks, hanging down below the shell. While the young are still in need of parental protection, they hide under this.

Armadillos may not look appetizing, but under their armor plates is flesh that appeals both to other animals and to humans. They have more than one way of trying to evade such enemies. The three-banded species of the Argentine pampas rolls itself into a ball, a maneuver which thwarts some pursuers. Others depend on speed for safety; they can burrow into soft or loose soil with amazing rapidity.

The World of Monkeys

To most people monkeys are monkeys. And it seems that in this type of animal, the Old World and the New meet—inhabitants of the jungles of Asia and Africa matching those of the tropical forests of South America. Scientifically, however, this is not accurate. As far back as their history can be traced through fossils, these two groups have evolved separately. Those in South America apparently are descended from creatures that moved down through Central America, island-hopping across the Isthmus of Panama before the land bridge materialized. The Old World monkeys have a different ancestry. If there *was* a common ancestor, it must have lived at least fifty million years ago, and its remains have never been discovered. Today the differences between the two groups are clearly defined by type of teeth, nose structure, and tail. No Old World monkey has a prehensile tail; several American species do.

As monkeys at a zoo are usually the most popular of its residents, so in their native habitats they prove irresistible to explorers. William Beebe wrote in *High Jungle,* "On our expeditions we were never without a Capuchin Monkey. . . . . . They wind deep into our affections and finally break our hearts when we have to leave them."

Capuchins do better in captivity than any of the other American monkeys and, as a result, are the type most often seen in zoos. They rate high in intelligence, being compared in this respect with the chimpanzee of the Old World. They have been known to make "tools" of sticks or pieces of paper to rake up food, the better to eat it, and to solve problems of getting at food that is in sight but out of reach by first using one tool to obtain still another one long enough to secure the meat.

There are a number of species of capuchins, and these vary in coloring and kind of hair. All are similar in size—an adult measuring about two feet, exclusive of tail. The tails are fully furred, and are prehensile only to a degree. The animal can hang by its tail for limited periods but can not use it as an extra hand. Those living in northern South America, north and west of the Andes, have a simple kind of "hair-do," a rather hairless face that is light in color, and a light front. Otherwise the coloring varies from jet black to brown and sandy tones. In the Orinoco basin and part of the Guianas, the capuchins are more heavily built, with thick brown coats and heavy fur around the ears which gives the face a rectangular appearance. Some of them have tall crests over the ears or, in certain cases, one central peak over the crown. The capuchins are active by day and wander around the forests in small bands. The food they seek is varied—fruits, certain leaves, and small animals such as snails and insects.

The smallest individual on this branch of the family tree is the squirrel monkey. The average size of most of those that have

HOWLER MONKEYS

been observed is only slightly larger than the ordinary squirrel, but if one of them manages to survive to full maturity, it may be four times as big. Squirrel monkeys are numerous in forests that border the Orinoco and Amazon Rivers. They travel in large troupes, consisting sometimes of hundreds of members. In pidgin-English they are called "monkey-monkey monkeys." Like the capuchin they are insect and fruit-eaters. They make continuous croaking noises unlike that produced by any other mammal.

On another branch of the monkey's family tree is the tiny marmoset, with a squirrel-like body but with facial expressions

SAKI MONKEY

and "talking" ability surpassing even that of the "squirrel"—or any other monkey. Since South America was first discovered, these little animals have been the most popular of all exotic pets. A marmoset's eyes are set far apart on its face and it has very human-looking ears. They are not usually seen, however, being covered by long, plumelike fur which falls smoothly back over the head, forming a mane. While other New World monkeys give birth to one baby at a time, the marmoset usually produces twins, and occasionally triplets. Also unusual is the fact that the father cares for the tiny infants, carrying them about all day except for feeding time when he hands them over to the mother.

Woolly monkeys are considerably larger than marmosets but they, too, make gentle pets. They are fairly common today in the forests of the upper Amazon and Orinoco Rivers. They are not to be recognized by color, because this varies with different types, but the kind of coat is consistent in all with very thick, woolly fur. Their tails are long and fully prehensile; the face is naked of hair and the eyes are large and brown with a distressingly sad expression. Usually they travel in family groups of from twelve to twenty-five individuals but occasionally there are twice that many. For the most part they live on fruit, although at certain seasons they hunt small vertebrates and also munch flowers and leaves.

The howler monkeys are strictly vegetarian. Often they spend six hours of the day cramming leaves, fruits, nuts and seeds into their mouths, grabbing the food in their hands as they swing from a strong prehensile tail. Howlers have the widest range of any of the American monkeys, extending from southern Mexico to Paraguay and tropical Argentina. The name "howler" was not bestowed on this creature without good reason: its voice is the loudest of any New World monkey, and it is said to be among the noisiest of animals anywhere, for its size. Ivan Sanderson wrote about the vocal outpourings of a group of howlers: "They sound like the roll of distant thunder preceded by the death-agonies of half a dozen tortured jaguars." But in spite of their deplorable voices, the howlers are admired by those who see them as handsome, even magnificent animals. They still exist in sizable numbers, but have been hunted enough to make them extremely wary of humans.

5

Climbers, Stalkers and Browsers

MONKEYS HAVE A variety of neighbors in their arboreal homes. One of these is the kinkajou which is often mistakenly called a monkey. It does have a resemblance to the monkey tribe, and like many South American monkeys swings through the trees with the aid of a prehensile tail. It also is commonly called a "honey bear," but it is not a bear either; instead it belongs to the raccoon family. Kinkajous have coats of short, soft thick fur which varies in color, some being gray, some yellowish. One native of central Brazil is rich chocolate brown with a cream belly. These animals are extremely fond of honey, and devote themselves to hunting bees' nests, extracting the honey from them with their long, narrow tongues.

The kinkajou's cousin, the coati or coatimundi, lives on the ground, but is an excellent climber. The raccoon-like animals travel about in bands—sometimes large, sometimes small—and when they invade a new area, they comb it thoroughly in their quest for food. Tree tops are searched, and so is the ground below. They will manage to walk a tightrope if it leads to something edible.

There are two principal types of coati. One is found from North America to the west coast of South America. The other ranges from Panama to southern Brazil. A coati is truly a "nosey"

creature. Its snout is so long it can be twitched about to an angle
of forty-five degrees!

Another relative of kinkajou and coati is the crab-eating
raccoon—a long-legged, colorful beast. Its fur of rich brick red
is trimmed with a black mask, white muzzle, vividly ringed black
and white tail, and white-fringed ears. Its chief habitat is the
Amazon Basin, but it extends north to Venezuela and Colombia
and south to the southeast coast of Brazil and Paraguay. It is
semi-aquatic and usually hunts such foods as crabs, shrimp and
frogs in the rivers. If hunting there is unsuccessful, however, the
night-prowling raccoon will turn to forests and gardens for fruits,
small birds, insects and sugar cane.

COATIMUNDIS

Early in the Age of Mammals, South America had a flourishing variety of marsupials. However, these pouched animals gradually lost out in competition with the placentals which nourish their young in the mother's womb until they are in an advanced state of development. One marsupial that did not succumb to competition was the opossum. It not only survived, but extended its range into North America. Today there are ten different kinds flourishing in the South American tropical rain forests. Among them is the four-eyed opossum, so-called because of a bright white spot over each eye. Far from "playing dead" as North American opossums do to protect themselves, it is fiercely aggressive. It spends much of its time in the trees and is a skillful catcher of small birds. The mouse-opossums are the most appealing in looks. Their fur is almost as silky as that of a chinchilla, and is rich brown on the back, and white or yellow underneath. The babies are about the size of a grain of rice; an adult is no bigger than a large mouse.

Rodents — Small and Large

The real mice of South America are an amazingly varied group. There are species that flourish in the swampy lowlands of the Amazon and others that thrive in high altitudes of the Andes, with many others in between. The various species include swimmers, tree climbers and diggers, as well as those that graze and browse.

Another small rodent living in the mountains of Ecuador and Colombia is a species of paca that makes extensive burrows and accumulates fat during part of the year. Then it goes into semi-hibernation in the cold, wet season. The larger pacas, which belong to the lowlands, are often seen exhibited at fairs and circuses as "curiosities"—perhaps labeled "the largest rat in the world." A fully matured paca, may have a length of well over two feet; actually it is the world's second largest rodent, and is distinguished by rows of white spots which line its flanks. These pacas are aggressive fighters, yet make agreeable pets. They have been called "animated garbage pails" because they eat enormous amounts of anything they can get their teeth into.

The largest rodent in the world is also a South American resident. This is the capybara—a popular exhibit at zoological parks. An adult may measure almost four feet over the curve of the back from muzzle to tail, and at least one individual on record achieved a weight of two hundred and twenty pounds. Capybaras somewhat resemble gigantic guinea pigs, but their bodies are clothed in very coarse bristles rather than soft fur. They have frightening teeth, a couple of inches long and as thick as a man's finger. Yet they eat only vegetation and when captured they are amiable, showing no disposition to use the teeth as weapons. The Indians use capybara

PUMA

teeth as chisels, and the animal's flesh is considered a good food, as is the case with that of almost all South American rodents. The capybara moves with a peculiar shuffling walk or a rolling gallop on land. It can swim and dive with ease and skill.

The big cats—jaguars and pumas—receive almost more than their due share of publicity because they are so very photogenic. However, they do not typify South America as do the rodents that developed there. The cats were among the later immigrants to cross the land bridge from the north and, except for puma and panther, their family did not produce especially interesting members. The easily-noticed difference between these two is in the color of their coats. Jaguars are spotted; pumas are a solid color of pale gray to sandy brown, with a spot of white at the chin. Jaguars are tropical animals, and the spotted fur serves as protective camouflage among the dense trees. Pumas also inhabit forests to

SPECTACLED BEAR

some extent, but their range is wide, throughout savanna country and mountains. Both cats stalk and kill other mammals and birds. The jaguars are also fond of river reptiles and fish, which they swish out of the water with a quick flick of the paw. It is not unusual for one to tackle a caiman, leaping on its back and breaking its neck. Because they also prey on cattle, they are ruthlessly hunted by ranchers and they are becoming increasingly rare.

Exclusively South American

The dog family in South America is distinctive and varied. There are no true dogs or wolves, but a number of animals that may be considered mixtures of such canines as dog, wolf, jackal and fox. The maned wolf, for one, is more fox than wolf, and its legs are so long they seem to belong to neither animal. It is exceptionally shy, and is on the prowl only at night searching for small animals and certain wild fruits. There are several wolflike species ranging through the bleak lands of southern Chile and Tierra del Fuego. One that formerly lived on the Falkland Islands, off the Patagonian coast, has been completely exterminated by farmers because it was attacking their sheep. These animals were so friendly to people they would lick the hands of those about to kill them.

Extremely rare is the bush dog, which is only distantly related to most other living canines. Its range is from Panama south to Brazil. Bush dogs are seldom seen in the wilds, but it is known that they hunt in packs of about a dozen individuals and that they are good swimmers. They are long-bodied and short-legged, standing about a foot high at the shoulder. Occasionally one is raised as a pet. Living with a human family, it acts very much like a dog— showing obvious enjoyment when its ears are scratched or its belly rubbed, or when a stick is thrown so that it can retrieve it.

An exclusively South American mammal of the present day is the peccary. It is piglike but not a true pig. Peccaries once lived also in Europe and Asia, but are now represented on those continents only by fossils. They resemble the European wild boar. The larger of the two species is fierce and aggressive; the smaller—the collared peccary—is milder in nature and when kept as a pet, proves intelligent and friendly.

Another South American "exclusive" is the spectacled bear— the only bear that does inhabit this continent. It lives high in the Andes Mountains of Chile and Bolivia, and has the un-bearlike habit of making a nest of branches and leaves. It is a rather small, shaggy animal, black, with eyes encircled by yellow rings that are the reason for its popular name.

The Hoofed Mammals

Unlike these unique animal forms, the deer family is represented by a number of types that have many relatives on other continents. The marsh deer of the wet lowlands in the Amazonian Basin are the largest of the South American species, matching our North American deer in size. They are distinctively colored; a lustrous red coat with white underparts is set off by black stockings. The smaller pampas deer on the southern savannas and pampas of Brazil, Paraguay, Uruguay and the Argentine are also reddish in color with white trimmings. The tail is black above and white below. This deer is extremely fragile in appearance but is a tremendous jumper, and when frightened can leap over ten-foot high clumps of pampas grass toward safety. The brocket, another deer of the Amazon Basin, has a habit unusual for deer. It sleeps during the day, coming out from holes and arbors of fallen trees in the evening to browse through the night. Nevertheless it is successfully hunted as food and for leather which is made into saddles and shooting bags.

The smallest deer in the world are the pudus which live at high altitudes in Peru and Ecuador and range south to temperate forests at the tip of Chile. The males are about the size of terriers; the females are even smaller—barely twelve inches tall. Laws presumably protect the deer during certain seasons, but they are not well enforced, and mothers with young are as likely to be slaughtered as any other.

In contrast to the pudu, smallest of South American hoofed mammals, the tapir holds the record as the bulkiest. It stands nearly forty inches at the shoulder and weighs several hundred pounds. Millions of years ago, tapirs were world-wide in distribution but today, besides one species found in southeast Asia, the only survi-

MARSH DEER

vors are those of South and Central America. The Brazilian species is the most common, ranging over much of the South American continent. A smaller woolly species frequents the slopes of the Andes, to heights of fifteen thousand feet. Whether in mountains or in forests, tapirs always live near ponds, lakes or streams. They are expert swimmers, and when frightened rush for the water at top speed. Often they reach it by sitting on a river bank and sliding down as if propelled on a toboggan—a performance that eventually wears the hair off their "seats." Their natural enemies are the jaguars, but people find them good eating, too, so that they are hunted to a considerable extent. Like fawns, the young have camouflage markings but as they mature, the patterned coat gives way to a solid brownish color.

Another hoofed mammal, the llama, is the animal that best represents South America to many people. As was noted in Chapter 2, llamas have been domesticated for generations; they no longer belong in the wildlife category. The alpaca, a close relative that shares the prehistoric camel as an ancestor, also has been domesticated for centuries. However, there are two other New World camels which still are wild—the guanaco and the vicuña. The story of the vicuña's rescue from extinction is told in Chapter 10. Guanacos, ancestors of both llama and alpaca, have managed to flourish through the years. They still live in large herds, roaming from the plains of Patagonia to the high Andes.

6

The Most Amazing Birds

ON SOME OF the earliest maps of South America, Brazil was called "Land of Parrots." Explorers had taken back to Europe a number of macaws, and their brilliant coloring and incredible voices deeply impressed everyone who saw them. Today people are still impressed by them and by all other parrots. The beauty of their plumage and their ability to mimic human talk, make them glamor birds without rival.

Parrots are only one example of the amazing birds native to South America. The hoatzin, a primitive bird and one of the few birds in the world with eyelashes; the harpy, heaviest of all eagles; the jabiru, biggest of all storks; the largest hummingbirds in the world and some of the smallest—these are a mere sampling of the distinctive bird life. Almost two-fifths of all known species in the world are represented from Tierra del Fuego to Mexico. This remarkable diversity is due in part to the variety of habitats—tropical rain forests, grassy pampas, the rocky mountain heights, and cold antarctic areas.

Compared with the mammals, birds have survived well since man's arrival in South America. Though a number are killed for food and for their beautiful feathers, the hunting of them is difficult and most kinds are too small to compensate for the effort involved. But as cities, towns and ranches continue to grow, there is a constant diminishing of the habitats that birds must have for survival. As with all other wildlife, their existence is threatened unless constant vigilance assures sanctuaries where they can breed and live in comparative peace.

Among the most hunted has been the rhea—a defenseless creature whose only hope of escaping pursuers is to run. It is flightless, like its cousin, the African ostrich, and its size makes it an easy target. Once it was numerous on the Argentine pampas. The Indians appreciated rheas as food. As they had to pursue the birds on foot, catching one was not easy. It was speedy, and had a habit of doubling back on its tracks, then falling flat in the tall grasses completely out of sight. For the past hundred years, the rhea has been desired for two reasons besides food: its feathers for dusters, its hide for rugs. And gauchos learned to ride down the birds on cow ponies, lassoing them with a bola—a leather thong with weighted ends which entangled the legs and neck. The rheas began to suffer also as the pampas changed from free, open country to areas of cattle ranches and wheat farms.

COCK-OF-THE-ROCK

HOATZIN

Beauty on the Wing

Far more remote from people are the birds of the so-called "cloud forest"—an area from two to three thousand feet up the Andean slopes. Here the moisture in the rising warm air suddenly cools and condenses, resulting in perpetual fog. And here colors run rampant in the native birds, among them hummingbirds and members of the trogon family.

All species of trogon are spectacular in their brilliance, the males varying from metallic or golden green to violet on the upper parts, and from bright reds through oranges and yellows below. One of them, the cock-of-the-rock, is startling in its beauty and its feathers are prized highly. In gorgeous attire it rivals a close relative, the quetzal, which was worshipped by the Aztecs and Mayas as the god of the air, and whose plumes were used in Aztec religious ceremonies. A remarkable habit of the cock-of-the-rock is its ceremonial dancing. A group of males and females congregate around an area which they clear for the purpose. Then, one by one the males take turns on the "dance floor," stomping about in a variety of improvised steps and stretching their wings, while the onlookers screech their appreciation.

Hummingbirds flash through the cloud forests like brilliant gems to which wings have been given. The "Andean rainbow," for example, has glittering patches of ruby and violet on its head, a golden throat, a violet bib and a cinnamon-colored tail decorating its greenish body. Of course, hummingbirds are not confined to this region. They live at still higher altitudes—up to sixteen thousand feet—and on down to the swampy rain forest, being most plentiful in the subtropical zone of Ecuador and Colombia. They are exclusively American birds; three hundred nineteen species of them are known. Of these, one hundred thirty-three are native to Colombia and Ecuador. By contrast, the United States has only eighteen. Among the various species is every imaginable type of bill, all shaped to fit into one kind of flower or another, from which the little birds can sip nectar. In doing so they act as dispensers of pollen. They are almost the only birds of the New World that fill this role, which is mostly handled by insects.

Dawn and sunset are the only times certain hummingbirds are active. In fact, this is true of many birds, and more than one explorer has been crestfallen to find a tropical forest apparently empty of inhabitants. But as day turned to evening and night to dawn, he would find a host of birds pursuing their various ways of life. Parrots are among those that fly by day. However, it is not always easy to see them, either, for their flying is done above the treetops as they move from one feeding area to another. Otherwise they stay high in the upper canopy of leaves.

MACAWS

HUMMINGBIRDS

TOUCANS

Parrots are not exclusively birds of the South American tropics, their greatest array being in Australia and New Guinea; but
there are enough of them in South America to be an outstanding
part of its bird population. The most talented talkers of the New
World all belong to the *Amazona* genus. They are largely green,
stockily built, and somewhat larger than a street pigeon. They are
prize catches when young, for they usually grow into talented
mimics.

Macaws are exclusively birds of tropical America, but zoo visitors the world over are often treated to a sight of them. The sickle-
shaped bills of these amazing birds are so huge as to look unwieldy,
yet with them, aided by a prehensile tongue, the macaws can crack
hard Brazil nuts and extract their meat. Among the largest of macaws is the "red-and-green" which is vivid scarlet and green with
touches of blue. It is common from Panama to Brazil, nesting in
high cavities of forest trees.

Smaller members of the family are the parakeets. One of them,
the monk parakeet of Argentina, has the unparrotlike habit of con-
structing a large, communal nest of sticks—a kind of crude apart-
ment house. For the most part, parakeets nest in cavities of trees,
termite nests, and earthen banks. There are still a goodly number
of these birds which travel in immense flocks, but they serve as a
reminder of their North American relative, the Carolina parakeet,
which has disappeared during the present century. They also were
numerous, highly sociable, and beautiful. They were hunted to
extinction.

Like parrots, toucans are widely known as pets. At home in
the tropical forests, they are among the most spectacular of all
birds. The enormous bill, almost as large as the creature it adorns,
is often brightly colored, as is the plumage, with much blue, yellow, red, orange and black. Toucans travel in flocks descending like
a robber band on a chosen area. While some take sentry duty, the

PARAKEETS

rest feast on the eggs and babies of other birds, and on fruits and berries. Their raucous cries ring through the forest, carrying for at least half a mile.

Because South America is inhabited by many birds that are non-singers, the impression is sometimes held that singing birds are rare on this continent. But there are song birds in delightful variety, many being similar to those of North America. Orioles, thrushes, warblers, tanagers, and buntings are a few of them.

Although any bird is likely to interest natives as food, and the feathers of colorful species are often desired for ornamental dress, the forest Indians are apt to show an intelligent regard for this kind of prey. For example, if only a few feathers are desired, the hunter uses a blunt arrow which merely stuns the victim. He then carefully plucks the feathers he wants, and sets the bird free.

The World's Rarest Breakfast Eggs

High in the Andes of Bolivia is a lake that provides a refuge for an extremely rare flamingo. All flamingoes are amazing—with their elongated legs, snakelike neck, and peculiar bill. But one species, thought for many years to be extinct, seemed especially intriguing because of unusual markings, including a red eye mask. It is called the James flamingo in honor of a British scientist who first captured a specimen more than a hundred years ago. After that none of these was seen for decades; then a Chilean expedition caught sight of a flock on Laguna Colorado, more than thirteen thousand feet up the Andes slopes. Encouraged by this report a team of zoologists and photographers left the United States in an attempt to photograph the birds, and if possible, to bring a few back to the New York Zoological Park. After an arduous journey and long searching, they discovered the flamingoes amid rows of mud nests, strung out on low islands. On some nests eggs were being incubated, but many were empty. The explanation for this lay close by: Indians living in caves raid the nests every two or three weeks for food. Apparently the only reason any eggs are spared is that these South Americans like their eggs to have a delicate taste. They give them the "float test," putting them in water: An egg that has been laid very recently sinks, a well-incubated one floats. Older eggs are replaced on the nest, and being touched by human hands usually does not harm them. The parents resume the incubation.

The explorers did not succeed in persuading the Indians to give up their egg hunts. However, they were able to capture a dozen of the flamingoes and successfully transport them to the zoo in New York. The birds quickly became tame, and adapted easily to their new life and surroundings.

Flamingoes are an ancient offshoot of a family group comprising ducks, geese and swans. Of the six known species, four are native to South America.

The eyelashes of the hoatzin are not the only unusual feature of this extraordinary bird. When a baby is hatched, it has claws on its wings; these fall off when the wing feathers grow in. Though the young chick is almost naked of feathers and looks helpless, it gets around remarkably well a few hours after birth. It crawls and moves through the trees like an accomplished acrobat, sometimes diving into the river from an overhanging branch and swimming under water to escape danger. After its feathers have grown, it can fly, but not very well. Each landing resembles an accidental crash more than a planned maneuver.

A bird that vividly illustrates the dependence of one kind of animal on another is the antbird, an inhabitant of the forests of the New World. It is found nowhere else. Antbirds were given their name because of some species which derive their livelihood from swarms of army ants. Not that they eat the ants! They follow along with the "army," and as the insects flush all kind of small creatures out of their hiding places on the forest floor, the birds dive to get at the victims first. There are certain other birds that also resort to this indirect hunting scheme, but the antbirds are the only ones to depend on it exclusively. A flock stays with the same insect swarm for a couple of weeks or more—as long as the ants are advancing and turning up new food. When the insects cease activities for a while, the antbirds at once look for another column that is on the move, and go along with it. Other birds return to their normal way of feeding when the ants leave their home territory.

Ants and other insects are an important part of the wildlife of South America. They eat and are eaten; without them the balance of nature would be completely upset. There is beauty among them: brilliant moths and butterflies, jewel-like beetles, and the brightest of all fireflies. Some have unique kinds of camouflage: the glass-winged butterfly whose transparency makes it all but invisible, and the tree hopper, a bug that is identical in looks with the thorns of the plant on which it lives. There can be danger from insects, too—most notably from mosquitoes which flourish in tropical rain forests as nowhere else in the world.

7

In and Out of the Water

EVERYTHING FROM mermaids to monsters can be found in South American waters.

This is a true statement of fact, but the "mermaids," on close examination, prove to be bald and wrinkled cow-like manatees, having little resemblance to the lovely creatures of man's imagination that were inspired by glimpses of these water mammals. And "everything . . . . can be found" may soon be only wishful thinking, as one creature after another becomes a rarity.

Manatees are not among those actually in danger of extinction at this time, but their numbers are drastically reduced. Several years ago the Amazon River, where many of them lived, fell to an unusually low level, with the result that the animals were easy to find. Hunters began to spear them by the thousands, selling them principally for their fat, which was boiled down and canned in huge drums. Despite this slaughter, the unique mammals survived. Today they are killed by Indians chiefly as food. Those that live in the upper Amazon are fresh-water cousins of the so-called sea cows that inhabit the oceans.

The "monsters" of South American waters are represented by the crocodiles and caimans, whose role in the world of fashion is discussed in Chapter 10. A hundred years ago caimans were more monster-like than now, for many individuals of the Orinoco River

GIANT RIVER OTTER AND YAPOK

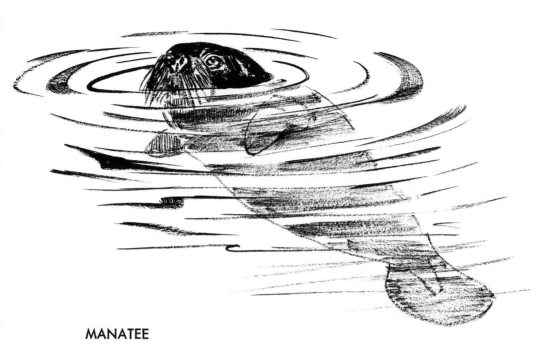

MANATEE

grew to a length of twenty feet or more. Today such giants are not to be found. The black caiman of the Amazon may attain fifteen feet in length, but the average length of these reptiles is between five and seven feet. The Orinoco crocodile is the biggest of its kind in the New World.

The animal of the Amazon river system that is probably its most intriguing inhabitant and also the one in most urgent need of protection is the giant river otter, *Pteronura.* This is the largest of all otters, growing to a length of six or seven feet. Like the smaller species, it is playful and easily tamed. Truly aquatic, it can stay under water for long periods of time, although it often stands upright, head above the surface, to look around. It has a great sense of curiosity. A canoe or launch, pulled on shore or anchored for the night, may have an unexpected visitor in the form of a dripping otter that has managed to wiggle its way over the side. The handsome fur of the Amazonian otter has been the cause of its unfortunate popularity with hunters and traders. Also its flesh is enjoyed by Indians as food.

As with other animals, the prices of skins indicate an abundance or a decline in numbers—and the amount paid for a single otter skin has risen from insignificant sums to at least seventy dollars.

One of the sights that most amazed Alexander Humboldt in 1799 was of dolphins swimming among the trees bordering the upper Orinoco, thousands of miles in from the sea where they normally are found. The situation was explained by the fact that the river was in flood—a quite regular occurrence with this stretch of water—and the animals were fresh-water dolphins. Today some still survive there—though not in great numbers—as well as in the Amazon Basin and the larger rivers of the Guianas. They swim near the water's surface in groups, often making long, graceful leaps as high as three or four feet in the air. Descendants of an ancient family of toothed whales, they have a bountiful supply of teeth in their long beaks. They can survive very well for a time in flooded forests, possibly miles from any river.

Another astonishing animal that spans the gap between water and land is the yapok, or water opossum. It is the world's only aquatic marsupial. Unlike other South American opossums that live among tree branches, the yapok has become adapted to river banks in wooded areas. Its home is a burrow at the river's edge. It emerges at dusk, and through the night dives for frogs, small mollusks and fish. Its feet are webbed like those of a beaver. The mystery about its odd existence is how the young survive. They stay in the mother's pouch as other marsupial babies do, and it would seem likely they would smother or drown during her constant underwater excursions. Obviously they do not.

The Dangerous Fish

Sharing the riverways with this assortment of mammals and reptiles are a fascinating variety of fish. One is the electric eel, the stranger-than-fiction creature which Humboldt encountered. Although electric eel is its accepted name, it is not a true eel. It is eel-like in appearance, but four-fifths of its long body is devoted to electricity-producing tissue. The vital organs of the fish are all crowded into the head end. Among these organs are neither lungs nor gills. Numerous small folds in the mouth are specialized for absorbing oxygen. The fish must come to the water's surface several times every hour or drown.

The electric eel is not the only potentially dangerous fish in South American waters. Among others are the sting rays. They belong to a salt-water group, but one entire family has adapted itself completely to life in fresh water, and its members are found throughout the Amazon-Orinoco systems. Totally unlike the cylindrical eel in shape, the ray has a flattened, disk-like body. Halfway down its elongated, flexible tail, is a spine with teeth like a saw. When anything or anyone steps on a sting ray, the fish quickly swings its tail up and around, driving the spine into the victim. Animals are usually easy prey after such an attack, and a person unfortunate enough to be so wounded usually suffers intense pain, swelling, dizziness and nausea. Sometimes death results.

Much smaller than the sting rays, but even more dreaded, are the pirahnas. They do not lie in wait for victims. They constantly rove through the water, ready to attack fiercely anything that comes their way. Some are no larger than a man's hand; other types grow to nearly two feet in length. All, however, have strong, triangular, razor-sharp teeth and powerful jaw muscles. There are four really dangerous species inhabiting a number of the streams that flow from northern Argentina to Venevuela. Wherever food is available, the fish gather and make short work of their victims, as many authenticated stories prove. For example, they may strip the flesh from a living hundred-pound capybara in less than a minute. Blood sends them into a frenzy; once it is detected they snap madly in all directions, even biting their own companions.

An incongruous relative is the pacus. This fish, though closely resembling a large pirahna in appearance, harms no living thing. It is a vegetarian, and subsists on fruit that falls from trees along the river banks.

The pirarucu, also called the paiche or the giant redfish, is unequaled as a source of food in the Amazon region. Today the average size of those caught is something less than five feet, with a weight of no more than a hundred-seventy-five pounds. But in the past, specimens caught were more often of nine and ten foot length, with a weight close to three hundred pounds. The pirarucu is usually speared or harpooned, then its flesh is cut into thin slabs to be dried in the sun. For three hundred years it has been hunted without restraint. Some degree of protection is now being given it by game laws, and the Brazilian government is attempting to establish it in ponds. It breathes air, and must surface regularly for oxygen.

A more unique air-breathing fish is the lungfish, which lives in swamps and rivers of Amazonia. It has a pair of nostrils that open from the exterior into the mouth, and although it also has gills, it must come up for air about every twenty minutes. When swamps or streams begin to dry up during the summer, the lungfish sinks into the mud and enters a hibernation-like state. As soon as rain falls, softening the hardened mud, the fish is aroused and resumes its usual activities.

Not all South American fish are unfishlike or dangerous. Some of the most beautiful little tropical fish, prized by home aquarium enthusiasts, are native to rivers of this continent. Brilliant species such as the *neon* tetra are usually found in clear, shaded forest streams. There are many species of so-called tetras, all less than three inches in length. They belong to the large fish group known as Characius. Another popular choice of tropical fish fanciers are the South American cats—little armored catfish, many of them having patterns of blackish spots, blotches or stripes on a lighter ground color. The "chocolate" cichlids often blush to a rosy pink. Such fish collected from the Orinoco and Amazon basins are an important export from South America. They are difficult to breed in captivity, but for the most part adults thrive on houseflies, dried shrimp eggs and mosquito larvae. Spinach makes an adequate substitute in the diet of the algae-eaters.

Betwixt and Between

Amphibians are creatures of two realms. Normally they lay their eggs in water; then as the young develop, they move out on to dry land. In South America some amphibians are different. Many have become tree dwellers and, while a number of these return to a lake or stream at egg-laying time, others have unique ways of surviving without going near these nurseries. There are frogs that attach their eggs to leaves situated over water so that when the tadpoles hatch, they fall in. With another kind, the great gray "marsupial" frog that lives on the steep mountainsides of Venezuela, eggs develop in a pouch on the female's back. When the froglets are fully formed, the pouch zips open and in a few seconds the babies jump out. Toads living in the Guianas also manage their eggs in this manner. There are frogs that show an interesting togetherness in producing their young. After a female has laid her eggs, her mate stays near them until they hatch. He then carries the tadpoles on his back to water. Some salamanders make use of water that collects in the cuplike base of *bromeliad* plants, both for egg-laying and to keep their skin moist.

Among other curiosities of South American amphibians are frogs that have no tongues; they sweep food into their mouths with long slender fingers. And there is the giant toad, *Bufo Marinus*, which may weigh as much as five pounds. It eats such a fantastic number of insects that it has been introduced to the West Indies, Hawaii and other islands as a check on insects destructive to plants.

Anacondas and Other Snakes

Reptiles are not dependent on water in the way most amphibians are; nevertheless there are a variety of them in South American rivers. Besides crocodiles and caimans there are turtles and snakes, including the mighty anaconda.

Anacondas definitely are river creatures—they are always found closely associated with water, often striking from there at prey on the land. They are excellent swimmers. However, they spend some time coiled around tree branches and may loop down on victims. They live on birds, caimans and mammals.

The anaconda may be considered almost a legendary animal. For generations fantastic tales have been told about it, with its size increasing every time a story was repeated. One quite recent report was of a sensational one-hundred thirty foot specimen, weighing over five tons, that supposedly was seen on the Amazon. Actually, an anaconda more than twenty feet long is rarely found today.

One good reason for the myths about super-colossal snakes may be traced to the practice of stretching the skins of dead reptiles. Herbert Dickey, a physician who spent thirty years in the various countries watered by the Amazon and Orinoco, tells of a man who dealt in snake skins and wished to oblige adventure-hungry tourists. He would soak a fresh snake skin with oil obtained from manatee fat, then leave it in the sun for a day. The following morning, he would attach it to a strong post on his house, and two men would pull on it until its length was doubled.

No exaggeration is needed, however, for the size of anacondas to be impressive. They are the largest snakes in the world. There is an authentic record of one with a length of thirty-seven feet, five inches. Anacondas are considerably larger than the boa constrictors to which they are closely related; the anaconda actually is one kind of boa. These reptiles are not poisonous, but kill their victims by constriction. In some forest areas, the native people have young boa constrictors as pets, for the snakes serve to keep an area relatively free of rats and mice. Gerald M. Durrell, recounting his experiences in British Guiana in *Three Tickets to Adventure*, describes coming to a village where "many of the children had young boa constrictors, beautifully colored in pink and silver and fawn, coiled round their waists or wrists. . . . They keep the boas in their huts and allow the reptiles the run of the place. . . ."

ANACONDA

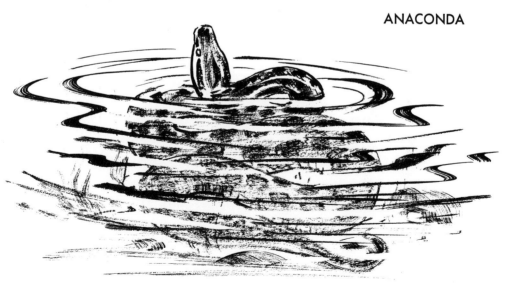

The most dangerous South American snakes are members of the viper family. Of these, the bushmaster is the longest. Its enormous fangs and large venom glands make it greatly feared— and with reason. There are a number of other, smaller poisonous snakes, including many species of coral snakes and one species of rattler.

More Reptiles — Large and Strange

Turtles may not catch as much popular attention as snakes, but some of those in South America are of especial interest to zoologists, and others have had great importance economically. The huge fresh-water turtle of the Amazon and Orinoco drainage systems has long served to feed the people living by these rivers. Such a turtle may weigh up to a hundred fifty pounds, or even more. Besides the meat being used as food, the eggs are valued as a source of cooking oil and for many other purposes. It is not surprising, therefore, that the numbers of the great reptiles have been diminishing rapidly. More than a hundred years ago, a medium-sized specimen could be bought for pennies; quite suddenly the price rose to several dollars. Today only the wealthy can afford turtle meat.

Protective laws, designed to save the turtles from extinction, exist in Venezuela and Brazil, but egg-stealing continues. During the wet season the turtles retreat to inland pools in the rain forests, later returning to their river habitats. The dry season gradually reduces water levels, and when they are at their lowest, the turtles crawl out on sand bars to lay their eggs.

There are other reptiles that help make South America a storybook land, and also serve a practical purpose in providing food. Among these are the iguanas, lizards looking like miniature dragons and tasting like delicate chicken. The largest species may reach a length of six feet or more, including its long tail. Iguanas usually live near water, and they are excellent swimmers. Often they drop from a tree top, crashing down through its lower branches and into the river with a mighty *plop*.

IGUANA

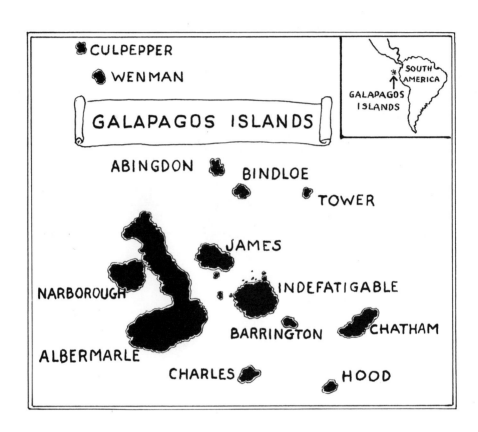

8

Galápagos—A Laboratory
for Evolution

"ENCHANTED ISLES" AND "Garden of Eden"—these were two of the
poetic names given at various times to the Galápagos Islands. But
such names are misleading. Few places on earth have a more
tragic history of untimely death and destruction, involving both
people and wildlife. Their official name, Galápagos, fits them best,
since it is a word that concerns tortoises—animals that once
abounded on these unique bits of land, six hundred miles off the
coast of Ecuador. In medieval Spanish, a concave shield used to
protect a soldier's head was called *galápago*. The tortoise with a
rounded carapace, being reminiscent of this, inherited the name.
And so, in the course of time, did the islands with their enormous
tortoise population.

"Enchanted" was a name bestowed more in frustration than
in admiration. In 1550 a Spanish sailing vessel trying to reach land
came close to the islands, only to have them disappear from sight.
The sailors did not know it, but their ship was caught in the un-
predictable currents of the Galápagos Sea. For days it was shifted
about, with the illusive land coming close many times only to
vanish again. Finally the sailors were convinced that the islands
themselves were moving—floating in the sea—and the ship's captain
called them *Las Encantadas*. The name "Eden" stemmed from the
remarkable lack of fear and shyness among the native animals

when they encountered humans. Even the abuse they have suf-
fered from people since the islands were first discoverd has not
entirely changed this. Dr. Eibl-Eibesfeldt, a scientist now involved
with conservation of wildlife on the Galápagos, tells of a trip there
in 1957 when he was able to stroke the fur of the sea lions. And
as he sat on a sand dune, a mockingbird came up to tug at his
shoelace, evidently coveting it for nesting material. Other birds
perched close enough to him to be touched.

This account does, indeed, give a charming picture, but one
that is unrealistic, since the popular image of Eden is of a beautiful,
inviting garden of plenty. For a classic description of the true
appearance of the Galápagos, we may read Herman Melville:
"Take five and twenty* heaps of cinder dumped here and there in
an outside lot; imagine some of them magnified into mountains and
the vacant lot the sea; and you will have a fit idea of the general
aspect of the Encantadas. . . ."

Of course, the islands were not "dumped." They were the
result of volcanoes that erupted deep down in the Pacific Ocean.
The volcanic cones rose above the water's surface, gradually
cooled, and in time were crumbled by erosion until some areas had
a meager soil. After that, when spores of certain plants were carried
by winds from the nearby continent and fell on the islands, it was
possible for them to take root. In time the "heaps of cinders" had
vegetation all their own, and while the areas close to the sea
remained desertlike, on the higher altitudes vines and grasses began to flourish. The islands were ready to support animal life.

Exactly where the fauna came from, and how the creatures
reached the Galápagos, no one can say for certain. But it seems
that as far back as the Age of Reptiles a number of animals must
have set out from the South American continent—without benefit

* actually there are only twenty-two islands, not twenty-five

of any land bridge—to seek new homes. Probably many made the effort without being successful, but some—such reptiles as giant tortoises and lizards, and a variety of birds and insects—succeeded. These immigrants, having established their own new world on the archipelago, proceeded to live in unique isolation.

Over the rest of the earth great changes were taking place. The Age of Reptiles gave way to an Age of Mammals; then people appeared on the scene, taking command of all living things. But for a long time even the explorers who were ranging far and wide did not know about the Galápagos and their wildlife.

It was close to the middle of the sixteenth century before a ship taking a high churchman from Panama to South America accidentally discovered these islands. Upon arrival at his destination he lost no time dispatching a report of his journey to Spain. The big news was, "We sighted an island. . . ." He then told of men going on shore for water and grass for the horses, but of their finding nothing but seals, turtles, iguanas like serpents, and tortoises so big that each could carry a man on its back. Further, his letter recorded, they landed on another island nearby where conditions were the same as on the first: "Many seals, turtles, iguanas, tortoises, many birds like those of Spain, but so silly that they do not know how to flee and many more caught in the hand. . . ."

Intriguing as the mysterious islands appeared to the Bishop, little interest in them was aroused in Europe. For a hundred years more they were still left peacefully to themselves. But then they became a meeting place for English buccaneers. One of the pirates wrote a detailed description of the animal life, commenting about the sea iguanas "they are so tame that a Man may knock down twenty in an Hours' Time with a Club." And "there are plenty of Turtle-Doves so tame that a Man may kill 5 or 6 dozen in a Forenoon with a stick." An unhappy foretaste of things to come!

IGUANAS

Pirates eventually gave way to other human invasions even more disastrous to the animal life. These were made by whaling ships, whose crews found fresh tortoise meat an excellent change of diet. They ate it while on land, and they stored as much as possible on board before setting sail again. One account written by a ship's captain mentioned that fourteen tons of tortoises had been collected in a single day. "We really could not stow away any more," he commented. During the War of 1812, the islands became strangely involved in action between the United States and Britain, and at various times fantastic characters settled on the rocky shores. They still belonged to no one.

It was in 1832 that Ecuador undertook to claim the Galápagos, an action which involved sending settlers to live there. The group of people who formed a colony on one of the larger islands at first seemed successful. Before long, however, there were revolts against the leader, followed by murders, and all kinds of disaster, and the settlement ended up as a political prison camp. The tragedy of all this to the native wildlife was that the settlers brought with them domestic animals. These inevitably became enemies of the natural fauna.

Thus the Galápagos Islands stood—poised between a remarkably long isolation from the rest of the world and a plunge into the chaos of commercial and political enterprises—when the young naturalist, Charles Darwin, stepped off the *Beagle* to continue his explorations there. The studies he was to make of the animals would, a few years later, furnish evidence for his theory of evolution. When he published *Origin of Species*, the eyes of the world were suddenly turned on the remote little part of the globe that seemed to hold answers to the mysteries of life itself.

9

Where Two Worlds Meet

NOT THE LEAST of the surprises of the Galápagos fauna is its combination of creatures of antarctic and tropical zones. Mingling with tropical reptiles are penguins that are native to Antarctica, the frozen continent at the bottom of the world. Also coming to breed on the shores of some of the islands are sea lions and fur seals.

The wide range of animal life results from a cool ocean current (often called the Humboldt) that comes up from the south along the coast of Peru and flows around the islands, modifying and changing its tropical temperatures. Another current—a warm one— that moves toward the Equator from December through February, converges with the cold Humboldt current, and the result is a season of ample rain falling on long-parched rocks and earth.

Reptile Giants

Sixty million years ago gigantic tortoises lived in many parts of the world; their fossil remains have been found in India, in southwestern United States, in Cuba and in Patagonia. And apparently they were numerous as well as widespread. However, since prehistoric times their habitats have dwindled to two groups of islands—the Aldabra in the Indian Ocean, and the Galápagos.

Giant tortoises are noted not only for the great size they attain, but for their incredible growth between infancy and adulthood. At the time a young one has developed its shell, its weight is about two and a half ounces. When fully grown, the individual may weigh five hundred pounds—an increase of four thousand times the original weight!

A female tortoise hollows out a hole and in it lays a large cache of eggs; the usual number is twenty. They are round and firm, closely resembling a billiard ball. When a cache is completed, the mother covers it with fifteen inches or more of the dry, crusty soil. Each baby develops in a folded position, its tiny head touching its tail. Its entire length is no more than two inches. After two months of incubation, it is ready to leave the eggshell confinement. It also must leave its below-ground nest, and this is no easy feat. Fifteen inches of earth, even though not very tightly packed, is considerable bulk to push through. Some of the little ones never make it, and die before escaping to freedom. Those that do succeed walk about their new surroundings dragging a tough egg yolk about the size of a fifty-cent piece which is attached to the under side of the shell. Gradually, during the course of a week or more, the yolk is absorbed into the body. It is believed that no other food is required during this period.

How a Giant Grows

After this, the young tortoise begins to eat coarse grass and such cactus pods as fall within reach. The ventral portions of the soft shell close, and the little reptile is ready to begin its adult life cycle. For many months, however, it could easily be mistaken for a typical land tortoise of North America, of the kind found commonly in woodland ponds. In two years the shell loses its flatness, in some species growing high and vaulted until its measurement across is as great as its length. Growth rate is quite rapid during

TORTOISE

the first twenty-five years. After that it slows to a mere half-inch a year. The shell of a fully grown individual measures about five and a half feet.

The manner in which the shell grows to keep pace with the tortoise body is interesting. The shell is not completely solid, but is made up of hard, bonelike plates which are separated by nerve centers. At certain times of the year the nerve centers turn white and, one by one, the plates drop out. Under each plate that drops, a new one—slightly larger—is waiting. As a result, the over-all shell extends as needed.

The great tortoises are creatures of daylight, and at dawn begin their daily search for food. On the lower slopes, this is largely cactus from which is obtained not only starch and sugar, but water. Those living on higher ranges eat moss and grass. During midday they look for a place protected from the hot sun so they can nap in comfort. On waking, they hunt food again until dusk, when they give their attention to finding a dry spot in which to sleep for the night.

During seasons when their island is plagued by a drought, tortoises climb to the higher altitudes seeking water reserves that lie in extinct volcano vents. They throw themselves into the water, then submerge their heads and rapidly gulp the liquid. All of this is not immediately absorbed into the system, and the excess is stored in a large sac within the carapace or shell, ready for future use. Unfortunately, pirates and whalers coming ashore on the islands discovered the existence of these secret reservoirs, and frequently killed the tortoises to satisfy their thirst without bothering to look elsewhere for water.

Only three hundred years ago, when the pirate ships began to call at the Galápagos, giant tortoises were numerous on all the islands. Even when Darwin stopped there, each island had some, and through them it was possible for the scientist to discover an important fact related to evolution: the tortoises of each island had certain distinctions from those of other islands; each separate species had evolved to suit its own particular environment.

In 1903 representatives from the California Academy of Science visited the Galápagos and found that tortoises were numerous on only three islands—Indefatigable, Albemarle and Duncan. On others they were either rare or extinct. Their slaughter by people and raids on the young by pigs, dogs, cats, rats and goats introduced by settlers, had taken their toll. The investigators saw, also, that on Albemarle the persecution was continuing. Enormous tortoises were being killed from which only a few pounds of meat and a bit of fat were taken. It seemed these survivors of prehistoric times must soon become extinct. But help is now being given to the reptiles and to other animals of the islands, through the Charles Darwin Foundation for the Galápagos Isles. The story of this excellent organization is included in Chapter 11.

The Little Dragons

The Age of Reptiles lives on not only in the giant tortoises, but in the Galápagos sea iguanas—the only living representatives of long extinct marine saurians. The males, gayly decorated with yellow and orange spots on a black background, have a row of spikes on the head and extending down the back that would do credit to any dragon. Their dark, short-snouted heads are encased in heavy plates, like armor, and the mouth when opened wide, shows a red tongue and lining. When two males are challenging each other over harems and territorial rights, they stand stiffly, raise the nape of the neck and the spikes, and every now and then squirt little streams of water from their nasal openings. This formal, rather gentlemanly type of combat is usually all that develops. The intruder coming on to property of an established male is apt to retreat after a certain amount of posing, squirting, and head bobbing. Sometimes a real fight does develop, but the antagonists seem reluctant to wound each other, which they could do quite easily with their sharp teeth.

Female marine iguanas "fight" in much the same manner over a disputed piece of ground. Sandy areas where eggs can be laid are often few and far between. The female digs a hole about a foot deep and in it deposits two eggs—all she will produce in a season. She covers them carefully, and leaves the nest with no further concern for protecting it. The females are somewhat smaller than the males, which attain an over-all length of four feet.

Although these reptiles are marine iguanas, they seem to prefer the land to water, and avoid swimming far out to sea. Their hind feet, though webbed, are not used to propel them when they do swim. This action is accomplished by the long tail which moves steadily from side to side. It could be that a fear of sharks keeps them grounded for much of the time; their remains have often been found in sharks' stomachs. They do go into the sea for their food, nibbling energetically at the plants there. For the most part they feed above water, but sometimes have a meal while well submerged, sitting among the coral rocks and meandering fishes.

The iguanas form one of the fascinating puzzles about the Galápagos fauna. Besides the marine species there are also land species, causing Darwin to comment that nowhere in the world except at the Galápagos would be found a genus having both its terrestrial and marine forms in so confined a portion of the world. The land iguana cannot swim, even if placed in water, and does not seem able to breathe under water.

These land reptiles live in deep holes which they hollow out by digging with their heavy claws. They feed chiefly on the cactus pods that drop to the ground, obtaining from them both water and nutriment. They are heavier bodied than the sea iguanas, the tail is shorter, and the head wider, although the snout is rather pointed compared with the blunt snout of their marine cousins. Their color varies between an intense yellow and brick red.

The scientific puzzle they pose is this: did the two kinds of iguana—marine and land—arrive at the Gálapagos as the separate forms they now are? Or did the land iguana evolve from the sea iguana? If not, how did the land iguana ever reach the islands? Its origin is unknown. There are no similar species to be found on the continents of South or Central America.

Seals and Sea Lions

Travelers have reported seals "haunting" the Galápagos for more than two hundred years. Until recently it was believed that they were of the same species as another that has an extensive range in southern waters. Then a close study revealed marked differences, making the Galápagos seals quite distinct. They were given a name of their own, *Zalophus wollbacki*. The discovery of a new species of mammal in the twentieth century was a noteworthy event.

Like other seals, they use the shore as breeding grounds and, after the young are born, as an open-air nursery. It is a lively place as the young play and tease each other while the males remain ever-watchful, each trying to keep the pups belonging to his own harem safe and peaceful. The females are inclined to be quarrel-

SEALS

some, easily stirred to fight over which bit of ground belongs to which. The males are alert to such commotions, and hasten to end hostilities.

Sea lions have longer limbs than the fur seals, and their necks are longer. They can turn their heads all about, and are very agile as anyone knows who has ever seen a "trained seal," which properly is called a sea lion. Many are shot by fishermen, who find them a nuisance. The fur of the fur seals that visit the islands is not so luxuriant as that of more northern seals. Nevertheless, they have been used recklessly by industry. Reports show that well over seventeen thousand individuals were killed on the Galápagos in a seventy year period in the nineteenth century. They are now extremely rare.

PENGUINS

FLIGHTLESS CORMORANT

Penguins of the Galápagos are considerably smaller than the mighty Emperor penguin of the Antarctic—in fact they are the smallest of all penguins, with a length of about twenty inches and a weight of five and a half pounds. They are the only penguins living entirely in the tropics. Likes those of Antarctic seas, they jump into the water and swim to catch food; they are entirely flightless.

Cormorants also hunt their food in the sea. However, most of them are able to fly, taking off from their roosting grounds to cruise over the water looking for fish. The Galápagos species is unique among cormorants in being flightless. Its wings are just a trifle larger than those of small penguins, and it waddles around in much the same manner as these birds.

There are a number of flying birds that compete for sea food—ducks, boobies, and swallow-tailed gulls—to name a few. In the

BOOBIES

ancient volcano craters where water has accumulated, and in lagoons, rose-red flamingoes stand, bending their long necks so they can scoop up insect larvae and other small creatures from the salty slush.

Such birds, beautiful and spectacular as they are, were not the ones of greatest interest to Darwin. It was the smaller, modestly colored finches that excited him, for in them he found evidence as important as the tortoises to his development of the evolution theory. Among the islands are ten distinct species—each different from all the others in size, shape of bill, method of eating and taste for food, so that there is no competition among them. After long study, Darwin deduced that all of these had evolved from a single species of ground finch, which ages ago was swept by winds from the mainland of South America.

Of the Galápagos finches, some have huge beaks suitable for crushing tough grain; the beaks of others are adapted for wood-boring, for probing into flowers, or for catching insects. One species is a remarkable bird that actually uses a tool to obtain food; the woodpecker finch secures a long thorn in its beak and with this, flushes insects from deep holes and crevices. When an insect is pushed into sight, the bird drops the thorn, grabs its victim, and then picks up its tool to go to work again.

Today fewer than two thousand people live on the Galápagos Islands. The Ecuadorian government provides schools, churches, mail service and medical care for them, but at best it is not a gracious place for human habitation. It seems designed to be a natural zoo with strange and significant wildlife, where prehistoric and modern times are brought together, and tropical and arctic zones are blended.

10

The Danger of
Being Fashionable

A SPECIES OF animal can disappear from earth very quickly if it catches the interest of fashion designers. The love· of beautiful plumes and feathers for hat and dress trimmings has led to the extinction or near-extinction of certain birds. A number of mammals, too, have been hunted relentlessly because their handsome fur coats were coveted by people. Even reptiles, particularly members of the alligator family, have been sacrificed to the whims of fashion.

In South America the caimans—so similar to alligators that only someone expert in anatomy can distinguish one from the other—and crocodiles are subjected to intensive hunting. When Humboldt and Darwin were exploring the continent, these reptiles were numerous enough to be quite frightening. Humboldt mentioned that they swarmed "like worms in the shallow waters of the (Orinoco) river." Today, the picture is very different. Reduced in numbers—in some areas, close to extinction—they need protection in order to survive. Their disappearance to a great degree is due to the popularity of alligator skin for making shoes, belts, handbags and wallets. Also, the young are captured to be sold as pets, unlikely and unlovely as they may seem for such a role.

The fate of the South American caiman has been tied in with that of the alligators of the southern United States. It was there the first wholesale raids on the great reptiles began, as alligator skin accessories became fashionable. Tourists enjoyed the novelty of bringing home a baby alligator, or shipping one to some unwary friend. Between 1880 and 1894 two million alligators were killed in Florida alone—but they still were plentiful. The hides sold for about ten dollars a thousand. By 1943 they had become so scarce that a single hide cost in the neighborhood of twenty dollars. About that time Georgia and the Carolinas passed laws prohibiting the killing or trapping of alligators. Shortly after, Florida made it illegal to kill them during the breeding season, and protection was further increased so that gradually the supply of skins in the United States dwindled to nothing.

The fashion world, however, was not to be thwarted; manufacturers turned to the South American caiman. No laws were protecting them there. In fact, the animals were generally feared and hated in their natural habitats because they ate anything they could catch and kill, and this sometimes included humans who got in their way. But few people will deny that they are fascinating survivors of the Age of Dinosaurs, and it would be a great loss if they were wiped out of existence. In some areas of South America where they once were abundant they already have been brought close to extinction. The killing and the trapping of young ones still goes on, but in the United States alligators are now being raised on farms in Florida and California exclusively for their skins.

There are mixed reactions to having alligators as pets. Many people who buy them in pet shops do so only to be different and soon lose interest in their welfare. But even those who are conscientious about keeping them healthy, find problems. 'Gators must be in a temperature of from seventy-five to ninety degrees at all times. And they must be kept in water deep enough so that they can eat while submerged. Few individuals survive being moved from hot, moist swamps to a cold tub or aquarium, though the change in environment can be accomplished successfully, if proper care is taken. Capt. John Edwards of Surrey, England, who happens to like and admire caimans and alligators keeps fifty or more in the basement of his home. Wanting to share his enthusiasm for the reptiles, he goes around the countryside on lecture tours, taking with him "Trudy," the largest of the caimans. A specially designed seat belt in his car allows her to travel in safety and comfort.

Luxury Coats

Another South American animal which has been a victim of high fashion more nearly fits the popular idea of what a pet should look like. This is the vicuña, resembling a small, humpless camel with exceptionally soft, silky hair. However, its charming appearance has not protected it from being slaughtered so that people could make clothing from its fleece. This is the ultimate in luxury

"TRUDY"

wool. Before the coming of Europeans, both the fleece and hides of these animals were reserved for the Incan rulers, their families and entourage, so that only a limited number were killed. The Europeans showed no such restraint.

Vicuña live in the remote uplands of the Central Andes, where each herd has a number of individuals that act as guards while they feed. Nevertheless, the hunters from the Old World found ways to outwit them. Great drives were held every few years, during which Indians were employed to frighten herds into an area where they could easily be killed. This custom, as well as other hunting, continued until the vicuña was all but exterminated. In 1940 the Peruvian government took action, passing laws which made illegal the killing of vicuña and the selling of articles made from its coat. Some poaching goes on, but for the most part, the vicuña wool available today is sheared from living animals, especially the males, which have a bundle of extraordinarily fine fleece hanging from the base of the neck at one season of the year.

As a result of this protection some vicuña can still be found in their top-of-the-world habitat. They flourish from twelve-thousand-foot heights on the Andean slopes as far skyward as any forage is to be found. Their lungs have a tremendous capacity. There is little oxygen in the air at such heights so that enormous amounts of air must be inhaled. The body must adapt, too, since the thin, dry air makes for rapid temperature changes, with the heat of the days giving way suddenly to extremely cold nights. This is where the beautiful, thick fleece serves its purpose, protecting the vicuña from both extremes. Anyone who regrets not being able to afford a vicuña coat can find solace in the thought that this unique creature needs it more than does any resident of town or country in the lowlands.

Two rodents, the chinchilla and nutria, also came dangerously close to extinction because the beauty of their fur caught the

COYPU (Nutria)

attention of the fashion world. The chinchilla fared the worst. After its discovery in the high Andes some fifty years ago, its pelts brought enormously high prices, and it was trapped unceasingly. Finally no more of the little animals could be found and the chinchilla was declared to be extinct. However, after a hunt of several years, an American engineer in 1922 managed to find fourteen live specimens. Using the utmost care, he succeeded in bringing them to lower altitudes and finally to the United States, in a refrigerated cage. Since then they have bred and multiplied until today there are in the neighborhood of seventy thousand living on chinchilla ranches, while some few still have their freedom in their native South American habitat.

Nutria, as it is known in the fur trade, is the coat of a rather large, aquatic animal which lives on both sides of the Andes, from

Peru southward almost to the tip of the continent. Its true name is the *coypu*. The nutria actually is the very fine underfur covering the body. It, in turn, is covered by a coat of long, coarse hair. When the numbers of coypu dwindled to the extent that hunting them was impractical, some were brought to the United States, where they continue to flourish in Louisiana, Mississippi and Texas.

Fortunes in Fertilizer

Fashion is not always concerned with clothing; it may be involved with other phases of life. Food, for instance, can be touched by whims of preference. And the way different kinds of things are produced or secured varies from place to place and from time to time. In farming, one always-important element is fertilizer; however, types of fertilizer also vary.

Guano, a remarkably good type, involves a dramatic story, one that is interwoven with the history of South America and its wildlife.

Guano is the excrement dropped from the countless birds—chiefly cormorants—that fly over small islands lying off the coast of Peru. The birds feed on fish such as sardines and anchovies that teem in the waters surrounding the islands, and the peculiar way in which this food is treated in their intestinal tracts gives the droppings an extraordinary value. It is thirty-five times as potent as ordinary barnyard manure! Besides its effectiveness when it is fresh, the climate enables it to retain its precious qualities over the years, so that the islands can be a real treasure trove—worth their weight in guano, rather than in gold. A complete absence of rain in the area accounts for the fact that the guano does not lose the ammonia and other mineral salts which make it particularly effective.

The value of guano was discovered by ancient Peruvian

Indians. The great terraces which the Incas built on the slopes of
the Andes for farming would have been quite worthless without
it, for the soil there was poor. With almost unbelievable effort and
enterprise, the Indians not only constructed the terraces but carried earth from the valleys to the high, sunny regions, developed
canals and irrigation ditches, and then imported guano. As a result,
their corn and potatoes flourished on the top of the Andes. The
Incas must have keenly appreciated their treasure, for they protected the guano islands zealously. Trespassers on them were
subject to the death penalty.

When the Spaniards moved into the land of the Incas, they
paid little attention to farming, for their great concern was gold
and silver. The resulting disruption of the Incan way of life meant
that Peruvian agriculture went into a decline. Guano was allowed
to accumulate, building up to a tremendous stock pile hundreds of
feet thick.

Then explorer Humboldt came to South America. When he
saw the islands with their great guano supplies, and realized how
valuable this fertilizer had been to the Incas, he knew he had an
important discovery. Ignoring the strong, unpleasant stench of
the bird dung, which provoked uncomplimentary comments from
his shipmates, he took a goodly supply back to Europe. There
it was tested and as it proved to be a truly remarkable asset in
growing vegetables, a guano boom quickly developed. The export
of guano to Europe gave Peru a new industry—one which involved
millions of dollars.

The people who were making fortunes from guano seemed to
have the illusion that its supply was limitless, perhaps because on
one island alone there was an estimated bird population of five
million. It was shipped out of the islands as fast as it could be piled
onto ships. And boys were paid to drive away the birds that were

producing fresh guano. The birds interfered with collecting opera-
tions! By the latter part of the nineteenth century most of the
islands were quite barren of their prize product.

In 1909 a unique conservation organization was formed—the
Peruvian Guano Administration (*Comparua Administrador del
Guano*). It was operated strictly as a business organization; stock
was issued, with high interest guaranteed. The sale of small
amounts of the guano still available was limited to agriculturists in
Peru and Chile. Exporting it to Europe was completely ended.
Controls were established on all the islands, with full-time wardens
on the job to protect the cormorants, pelicans, terns and gulls
which came there to nest. During the year 1911 it was difficult to
collect 30,000 tons of the fertilizer from the entire area. In 1938
168,000 tons were available for use.

The success of a conservation movement run as a business
enterprise, responsible to the government, continues. The greater
part of the guano sold each year goes to Peruvian and Chilean
farmers. And the birds, producers of a fertilizer that will never go
out of fashion, are given every possible protection.

11

While There Is Life....

"ALL THE KING's horses and all the king's men couldn't put Humpty Dumpty together again." No more can all the marvels of science bring back to earth any form of life, once it has been completely destroyed.

A long view of the earth's history reveals that animals can become extinct without being persecuted by man. The dinosaurs are an example; they lived and vanished ages before there were people. But their existence covered a span of *millions* of years; one theory suggests that they died off because of racial old age. Man's years on earth must be reckoned by the thousands. He inherited it as a wonderland of natural resources and wildlife, indescribable in their variety and beauty. Through countless generations this natural world did not suffer at his hands, but then trouble began. Increasing numbers of people, increasingly efficient methods of killing, increasing destruction of the natural habitats of wild animals—all started to take their toll. In the past two thousand years or less, about one hundred kinds of mammals and one hundred kinds of birds have become extinct—animals that had taken millions of years to evolve. If such slaughter should continue unchecked, the end of all wildlife could be anticipated in a not very distant future.

About three generations ago the situation began to alarm a scattering of people. Various countries and states had conservation laws, but they were inadequate and, for the most part, were not enforced. Some farsighted people who believed that nature's creatures belonged to everyone and deserved protection from commercial interests and wanton killers, launched a campaign for reforms. In the United States the establishment of Yellowstone National Park in 1872 was the first proof of Federal concern for conservation. Not many years later, President Theodore Roosevelt gave vigorous support to all suggested measures for preserving the nation's resources, including wildlife. At the same time a strong impetus was given a movement toward international nature protection, largely through the efforts of two men—Dr. William Hornaday in North America and Dr. Paul Sarasin in Switzerland.

Thanks to the rising tide of interest, a number of international conferences were held, at which representatives of many countries discussed ways and means of preserving birds, mammals and fish. In 1940 the Convention of Nature Protection in the Western Hemisphere came into being. Soon after, Venezuela, Guatemala, El Salvador, Haiti and the United States formed a pact to protect wildlife of the Western Hemisphere. They were later joined by Ecuador, Argentina, Peru, Brazil, Mexico and the Dominican Republic.

In 1948 a conference sponsored by France and Switzerland in association with UNESCO (United Nations Educational, Scientific and Cultural Organization) created an excellent wildlife protection agency. Known as the International Union for the Conservation of Nature and Natural Resources, it is dedicated to the preservation of man's natural environment. Its aims include the preservation of wildlife in all parts of the world, the promotion of conservation education and scientific research, and the preparation of international draft agreements for the protection of nature.

Among the noteworthy achievements of the International Union is the setting aside of large tracts of land in various areas of the world, called "The Last Refuges." One of them is the Rancho Grande Reserve of Venezuela, described by William Beebe in *High Jungle* as the ultimate cloud jungle, with mosses and lichens worthy of the best efforts of Walt Disney and Arthur Rackham. He also called it a little piece of all the world, with fourteen distinct, different zones—each worthy of a lifetime of study.

Dr. Beebe was not able to spend his life in even one of the zones, but he did devote three years to research in Rancho Grande. With his scientific staff he lived in the heart of the Refuge, housed in a fantastic castle which had been planned by Juan Vincente Gomez at the height of his career as President of Venezuela. The structure—an enormous three-storied creation with oval, semi-circular, rectangular, square and triangular rooms, joined together by intricate mazes of corridors—was nearing completion when Gomez died. Work on it stopped instantly, and there it stood for fourteen years, serving only as a highly unusual shelter for wildlife, until Dr. Beebe's arrival. Even then many of the animals stayed on within its confines. Keeping them out would have been difficult, even if Dr. Beebe had wished, because in some places the concrete roof gave way to open sky; some of the corridors had only wide-spread steel girders as floors; and many doorways were doorless.

The frogs, snakes, spiders, insects, birds, monkeys and other beasts sharing their domicile, did not daunt the scientists. However, it became necessary to confine a number of the animals to cages—and soon Dr. Beebe found himself the curator of a zoo that attracted countless visitors, from ragged urchins to government officials. Being host to such callers was time-consuming, but he welcomed everyone. Their coming provided an opportunity to dispel superstitions and misinformation about native animals, and often to learn from his guests.

NATIONAL PARKS

1. Kaieteur N.P.—British Guiana
2. Easter Island and San Juan Fernandez N. P.—Chile
3. Laguna de San Raphael N. P.—Chile
4. Cabo de Hornes N. P.—Chile
5. Pirihueico N. P.—Chile
6. Villarrica N. P.—Chile
7. Nahuelbuta N. P.—Chile
8. Henry Pittier N. P. (Rancho Grande N. P.)—Venezuela
9. Sierra Nevada de Merida N. P.—Venezuela
10. Guatopo N. P.—Venezuela
11. Yurubi N. P.—Venezuela
12. Avila N. P.—Venezuela
13. Alexander von Humboldt N. P.—Venezuela
14. Chaco N. P.—Argentina
15. El Rey N. P.—Argentina
16. Iguazu N. P.—Argentina
17. Laguna Blanca N. P.—Argentina
18. Lanin N. P.—Argentina
19. Nahuel Huapi N. P.—Argentina
20. Los Alerces N. P.—Argentina
21. Perito Francisco P. Moreno N. P.—Argentina
22. Los Glacieres N. P.—Argentina
23. Tierra del Fuego N. P.—Argentina
24. Rio Pilcomayo N. P.—Argentina
25. Itatiaya N. P.—Brazil
26. Rio de Janeiro N. P.—Brazil
27. Iguazu N. P.—Brazil
28. Cutibireni N. P. (Proposed)—Peru
29. Galápagos Islands N.P.—Ecuador

OF SOUTH AMERICA

The World Wildlife Fund Begins

The help that governments and individuals gradually began to give vanishing wildlife provided some protection, but still more was needed. In 1961 conservation-minded people of several countries made a general appeal for financial aid, and as a result the World Wildlife Fund was launched. This is now an organization of wide scope. It surveys all areas where wild animals are still to be found, and gives financial aid where it is needed to rescue a vanishing species. Recently, under the auspices of the World Wildlife Fund, Philip K. Crowe, former United States Ambassador, made an extensive trip through South America, viewing the national parks, visiting with heads of state, and talking with museum officials (who know what animal life used to be in their country) and zoo officials (who know what animal life exists now).

Mr. Crowe's extensive report on his mission discusses the progress that has been made toward conserving wildlife, the weaknesses of existing conservation programs and their prospects for the future.

Efforts to prevent the extermination of animals have varied in their effectiveness, Mr. Crowe notes. The protection of birds on guano-producing coastal islands of Peru is outstanding as a successful venture in conservation. National parks are a move in the right direction, but most of them are not really game sanctuaries. Shooting and lumbering are carried on in many; in others homes have been constructed for large numbers of people. Cattle may graze there. Even where great, virgin areas have been set aside, few wardens are employed to guard them from poachers. Argentina, with the largest system of national parks of any South American country, has four and a half million acres of reserves—but only fifty game wardens in its employ. Uruguay has fourteen wardens for some seventy thousand square miles of wildlife refuges. As a result, in the majority of nominal sanctuaries the animals are very much at the mercy of poachers. When an illegal hunter is apprehended, his fine is so small that he is not in the least discouraged from trying again.

One of the areas that has been given excellent attention is the British colony known as the Falkland Islands. They lie close to the southernmost tip of the continent, and on their shores may be found penguins and many other birds of sea and land, sea elephants, sea lions and a few fur seals. The wild animals there were not always given protection, and some people today may remember when the last native fox was shot, in the last century. Now, however, seventeen of the two hundred and two islands are becoming sanctuaries, and a six-months closed season for game birds is being considered.

Mr. Crowe's most urgent recommendations in the cause of conservation are toward education—perhaps beginning in the public schools. Some South American countries are introducing courses in the subject at teachers' colleges. If the citizens of the various countries come to understand the urgency of conservation, there is hope that the good laws will be obeyed without force, and that more laws will be passed where necessary.

A vital piece of work given financial aid by the World Wildlife Fund is the Charles Darwin Foundation for the Galápagos Islands. The Ecuadorian government, startled by the rapid diminishing of the notable animal life of this territory, in 1934 passed protective laws to save such creatures as the sea lion, fur seal and penguin. However, twenty years after these laws had been enacted, an expedition from Germany made a survey which revealed shocking facts. As Irenaus Eibl-Eibesfeldt relates in his book *Galápagos*: "Sea lions with bashed-in skulls lay rotting on the shores. Birds with broken wings and smashed beaks lay about. The sun-bleached armour of giant tortoises was mute testimony to the misdeeds of Man. . . . It was obvious that the law was inoperative for there was no one in all the islands whose duty it was to insure that it was respected."

Dr. Eibl-Eibesfeldt appealed to the International Union for Conservation of Nature and Natural Resources to take action, and before long he was requested by the Union and by UNESCO to select a site for a biological station in the Galápagos. The government of Ecuador gave its consent and complete cooperation to the project. After an extensive survey had been made, an area on the southern shore of Indefatigable Island was pronounced ideal for the purpose, and the Charles Darwin Foundation is now located there. Members of its staff hope to use it not only as an international research station, but as a base from which to reach out to guard the nature reserves of the archipelago.

So, in the dark picture of vanishing wildlife, there are hopeful glimpses. Governments have begun to recognize the tragedy of having their native animals exterminated, and an increasing number of private citizens are dedicating themselves to studying the birds and beasts, meanwhile arousing a popular interest in them. One such person is Augusto Ruschi who, largely at his own expense, developed a public wildlife museum in the mountain village of Santa Teresa, Brazil. Swarms of hummingbirds enliven the forest surrounding his home, which is visited each year by many thousands of people. When it became too difficult for him to devote his time to non-profit activities, the Brazilian government made a biological field station of his home and gave him the position of its manager—on salary.

Wildlife that is beautiful, exotic and exciting still is part of the South American scene, and if increased help is given to the creatures that are menaced by a rapidly changing world, there is hope for their survival.

Bibliography

Attenborough, David. *Zoo Quest to Guiana*. Thomas Y. Crowell Co. New York, 1956.

Bates, Marston. *The Land and Wildlife of South America*. Time Inc. New York, 1964.

Beebe, William. *High Jungle*. Duell, Sloan & Pearce. New York, 1949.

————. *Edge of the Jungle*. Duell, Sloan & Pearce. New York, 1950.

Bishop, Elizabeth. *Brazil*. Time, Inc. New York, 1962.

Butler, G. Paul and Erica. *Butlers' South America*. D. Van Nostrand Co. New York and Princeton, N. J., 1960.

Carbary, L. J. "All About Alligators." *Science Digest*. September, 1961.

Carlson, Fred Albert. *Geography of Latin America*. Prentice-Hall, Inc. Englewood Cliffs, N. J., 1952.

Colbert, Edwin H. *The Dinosaur Book*. McGraw Hill Book Co., New York 1951.

————. "Circus Without Spectators." *The Illustrated Library of Natural Sciences*. Simon & Schuster. New York, 1958.

Conway, William G. "In Quest of the Rarest Flamingo." *National Geographic*. July, 1961.

Coon, Carleton S. *The Story of Man*. Alfred A. Knopf. New York, 1945.

Darwin, Charles. *The Voyage of the Beagle*. Everyman's Library 104. New York, 1908. Also Doubleday Paperback, 1962.

Drimmer, Frederick (Editor). *The Animal Kingdom*. Greystone Press. New York, 1954.

Durrell, Gerald. *Three Tickets to Adventure*. Viking Press. New York, 1954.

Eibl-Eibesfeldt, Irenäus. *Galapagos*. Doubleday & Co. New York, 1961.

Gabel, Creighton. *Man Before History*. Prentice-Hall, Inc. Englewood Cliffs, N. J., 1964.

Gilliard, E. Thomas. *Living Birds of the World*. Doubleday & Co. New York, 1958.

Hudson, W. H. *The Purple Land*. E. P. Dutton & Co., Inc. New York, 1904.

Knight, Charles R. *Before the Dawn of History*. McGraw Hill Book Co. New York, 1935.

Life Magazine. "A Seat Belt for Trudy." May 24, 1963.

Lutz, Bertha. "Wildlife in Brazil." *The Illustrated Library of Natural Sciences*. Simon & Schuster. New York, 1958.

Matthiessen, Peter. *The Cloud Forest*. Viking Press. New York, 1961.

Milne, Lorus J. and Margery. *The Balance of Nature*. Alfred A. Knopf. New York, 1960.

Montague, Ashley. *Man—His First Million Years*. World Publishing Co. Cleveland and New York. 1957.

Pinney, Roy. *Vanishing Wildlife*. Dodd, Mead & Co. New York, 1963.

Rankin, A. "Augusto Ruschi's Garden of Eden." *Reader's Digest*. June, 1965.

Sanderson, Ivan T. *Living Mammals of the World*. Hanover House. New York.

Scheele, William E. *The First Mammals*. The World Publishing Co. Cleveland and New York, 1955.

Schmidt, Karl P. and Inger, Robert. *Living Reptiles of the World*. Doubleday and Co. New York, 1957.

Sick, Helmut. *Tukani*. Eriksson-Taplinger Co. New York, 1960.

Simpson, George Gaylord. "The Meek Shall Inherit the Earth." *The Illustrated Library of Natural Sciences*. Simon and Schuster. New York, 1958.

Tomilson, H. M. *The Sea and the Jungle*. Everyman's Library. E. P. Dutton & Co. New York, 1920.

Vogt, William. *Road to Survival*. William Sloane Associates, Inc. New York, 1948.

Von Hagen, Victor Wolfgang. *South America Called Them*. Alfred A. Knopf. New York, 1945.

———. *Ecuador and the Galapagos Islands*. University of Oklahoma Press. 1949.

Wiley, Gordon. "New World Prehistory." *Science*. January 8, 1960.

Index

Alligators, 97-99
Alpaca, 20, 21, 56
Amazon basin, 22, 25, 38; snakes of, 74-75
Amazon River, 31; fish of, 73
Amphibians, 73-74
Anaconda, 75
Andes Mountains, 2, 22, 37-38
Ankylosaurus, 13, 15
Antbird, 65
Anteater, 39-40
Aragua National Park, 37
Armadillo, 33, 34, 40, 41-42

Beebe, William, 37, 42, 107
Beagle, the, 32-36
Bear, spectacled, 52, 53
Bering Strait, 19
Birds, 57-66
Boa, 75
Bonpland, Aimé, 27-32
Boobies, 94-95
Brazil, Central Foundation, 38
Buntings, 63
Bushmaster, 76

Caiman, 67-68, 97-99
Camel, prehistoric, 14
Capuchin, 43

Capybara, 30, 50
Casiquiare River, 30
Catfish, 73
Cenozoic Era, 14, 16
Charles Darwin Foundation for the Galápagos Islands, 111
Chinchilla, 22, 100-101
Coati, 47-49
Cock-of-the-rock, 58-59
Cormorant, 93, 104
Convention of Nature Protection, Western Hemisphere, 106
Coypu, 101, 102
Crocodile, 14, 31, 67-68, 97
Crowe, Philip K., 9-10, 110-111

Darwin, Charles, 32-37, 84
Deer, 34; march, 54, 55; pampas, 54; brocket, 54; pudus, 54
de Godin, Isabela, 28
Dickey, Herbert, 74-75
Dog, bush, 53
Dolphin, 70
Dove, 81
Duck, 93
Durrell, Gerald M., 75

Egret, 35
Eibl-Eibesfeldt, Irenaus, 111-112

Electric eel, 29, 71

Falkland Islands, 111
Finch, 96
Fish, 71-73
Flamingo, 35, 64-65, 96
Frog, tree-dwelling, 73; gray
    marsupial, 73; tongueless, 74

Galápagos Islands, 36, 78-96
Galápagos, 111
Glyptodon, 16
Grison, 22
Guanaco, 26, 34, 35, 56
Guano, 102-104
Guinea pig, 20
Gull, 93, 104

Harpy, 57
High Jungle, 43, 107
Hoatzin, 57, 59, 65
Hornaday, William, 106
Horse, prehistoric, 15-16
Humboldt, Alexander, *see* Von
    Humboldt
Humboldt Current, 85
Hummingbird, 57, 58, 60, 61

Iguana, 76-77, 81, 82-83, 89, 90
Inca Indians, 20-21, 37, 102-103
Indefatigable Island, 112
Indians, forest-dwelling, 24; Inca,
    20-21, 37, 102-103; Ona, 25
Insects, 66
International Union for the
    Conservation of Nature and
    Natural Resources, 106-107, 112
Isthmus of Panama, 12

Jabiru, 57
Jaguar, 51-52

Kingfisher, 35

Kinkajou, 39, 47

Last Refuges, The, 107
Llama, 20, 23, 56
Lungfish, 72

Macaw, 61, 62
Mammals, Age of, 49, 81
Manatee, 67, 69
Megatherium, 16, 17, 33
Melville, Herman, 80
Mesozoic Era, 13
Mice, 39, 50
Monkey, 39; Old World and New
    compared, 42; capuchin, 43;
    squirrel, 43; marmoset, 45; saki,
    45; howler, 44, 46; woolly, 46

National Parks, located on maps,
    108-109; 110-111
Nutria, 100-102

Ona Indians, 26, 35
Opossum, 49
Origin of Species, 84
Oriole, 63
Orinoco River, 28, 30
Otter, giant river, 68-70

Paca, 50
Pacus, 72
Paiche, *see* pirarucu
Parakeet, 62, 63
Parrot, 57, 62
Patagonia, 20; fossils of, 33
Peccary, 53
Pelican, 104
Penguin, 85, 92
Peruvian Guano Administration,
    104
Pirahna, 71
Pirarucu, 72

piume, 30
Pizarro, Francisco, 21
Puma, 34, 51-52

Quetzal, 58-59

Raccoon, crab-eating, 48
Rancho Grande, 37, 107
Rat, 39
Reptiles, Age of, 13, 14, 81
Rhea, 34, 35, 58
Roosevelt, Theodore, 106
Ruiz, Hipolito, 28
Ruschi, Augusto, 112

Salamander, 73
Sarasin, Paul, 106
Sea cow, 67
Sea lion, 85, 92, 111
Seal, 81, 85; Galápagos, 91-92; 111
Sick, Helmut, 38
Skunk, 34
Sloth, 39-41
Snakes, 74-76
Smilodon, 17
South America, divisions of, 20
Spruce, Richard, 37

Sting ray, 71

Tanager, 63
Tapir, 30, 54-55
Tern, 104
Tetra, 73
Tierra del Fuego, 20, 25-26
Toad, 73, 74
Tortoise, giant, 79, 81, 85-89
Toucans, 61, 62
Toxodont, 17, 33
Three Tickets to Adventure, 75
Thrush, 63
Trogon, 58-59
Tukani, 38
Turtle, 14, 76, 81

Vicuna, 20, 56, 99-100
Von Humboldt, Alexander, 27-32, 36, 37, 103

Warbler, 63
World Wildlife Fund, 25, 110-111
Wolf, maned, 52-53

Yapok, 68, 70
Yellowstone National Park, 106